Meaningful Existence

A REFLECTION ON HEMINGWAY'S MAJOR NOVELS

by

OLIVIA CANCHELA VILLA-REAL

Gotham Books

30 N Gould St.
Ste. 20820, Sheridan, WY 82801
https://gothambooksinc.com/

Phone: 1 (307) 464-7800

© 2024 *Olivia Canchela Villa-Real*. All rights reserved.

No part of this book may be reproduced, stored in a retrieval system, or transmitted by any means without the written permission of the author.

Published by Gotham Books (August 27, 2024)

ISBN: 979-8-3304-0218-2 (H)
ISBN: 979-8-3304-0216-8 (P)
ISBN: 979-8-3304-0217-5 (E)

Because of the dynamic nature of the Internet, any web addresses or links contained in this book may have changed since publication and may no longer be valid.

The views expressed in this work are solely those of the author and do not necessarily reflect the views of the publisher, and the publisher hereby disclaims any responsibility for them.

FOREWORD

In my quiet moments, I look deep within myself, and I ponder on the transience of life and the purpose of my existence. Sometimes, it takes a tragic event in our lives to put our activities to a grinding halt and force us to answer questions which we have neither the time nor the interest to dwell on. These questions are basic to our existence, and they seem to be left unanswered and posed to us as a bitter pill we must swallow and face when a loved one leaves us behind through death. I have swallowed this pill more times than I would have liked with the death of my loved ones— my parents, my only brother, my husband, my uncles, and a few of my friends.

This book is based on a thesis that I wrote when I was in my twenties in compliance with the requirements for the degree of Master of Arts in English, which embodies Hemingway's philosophy of meaningful existence as I have seen through the lens of my Christian upbringing. Decades have passed from the time this was submitted as a master's thesis and life events, both big and small, have shaped my philosophy and understanding of how man must live his life to achieve a truly meaningful existence. And my philosophy continues to evolve, shaped by every pebble on the road I walk on in this mysterious journey of life! The colorful beads from the fountain of life will continue to appear on my horizon, enlivening my spirit to walk on when the roads prove rugged and unbearable. And this spirit, unbroken by circumstance, will continually shape the dynamic progress of my philosophy of meaningful existence until I reach the end of my journey.

DEDICATION

It is with deep gratitude that I acknowledge my indebtedness to the faculty of the Far Eastern University Graduate School whose scholarly and unselfish guidance has led to the completion of this study.

I also acknowledge my gratitude to the Graduate School Librarians and the Librarians of the United States Information Service who opened their treasure vault of information to enable me to complete this work.

Furthermore, I will forever be singing praises to my dearly loved father, Osmundo Canela Villa-Real, who diligently transcribed my handwritten work into its print format. His vigilance and unfailing support remained as the constant wind beneath my wings when my flight proved tortuous and challenging. To him and to my beloved mother, whose unfathomable love and devotion I will forever cherish, I solemnly dedicate the accolade from the completion of this study.

And as I release this book to the world in publication, my efforts are made more meaningful, my challenges more surmountable, and my aspirations more attainable, made sweeter by the presence of my loving family—Carl Edward Jacobsen, Marc-Anthony Villa-Real Alabanza, Bella-Olivia Villa-Real Alabanza, and Donna-Carole Villa-Real Jacobsen. This over-arching family tree that sustains and nourishes my spirit is strengthened by the presence of Kathya Alabanza, Darren Pfefferman and Jonathan Gray who have given the miracle of life to our tree's young, colorful twigs in Jonas Pfefferman, Emerson Alabanza, Kayla Pfefferman, Patajali Alabanza, Ethan

Pfefferman, Addison Gray, and Chloe Gray. All these wonderful people are like colorful beads that glitter to color our family tree of life.

O.C.V

TABLE OF CONTENTS

Title	Page
FOREWORD	1
DEDICATION	2
TABLE OF CONTENTS	4
INTRODUCTION	5
Chapter I — The Background of the Study	10
Chapter II — Meaningful Existence from the Christian Angle	24
Chapter III — The Hemingway World, His Concept of Life, of Morality, and of the Nature of Man	33
Chapter IV — Hemingway's Philosophy of Meaningful Existence	39
Chapter V — Hemingway's Philosophy of Meaningful Existence in <u>The Sun Also Rises</u>	43
Chapter VI — Hemingway's Philosophy of Meaningful Existence in <u>A Farewell to Arms</u>	75
Chapter VII — Hemingway's Philosophy of Meaningful Existence in <u>For Whom the Bell Tolls</u>	86
Chapter VIII — Hemingway's Philosophy of Meaningful Existence in <u>The Old Man and the Sea</u>	97
CONCLUSION	109
BIBLIOGRAPHY	130
PERIODICALS	134

INTRODUCTION

Prompted by a great enthusiasm to contribute to a fuller understanding of a world-known American writer whose advent into the field of literature had created a marked change in the twentieth century American fiction, I have chosen to publish this book entitled: MEANINGFUL EXISTENCE: A REFLECTION ON HEMINGWAY'S MAJOR NOVELS. Moreover, desirous to have a maximal feeling of its ethical value, I have undertaken the task of evaluating it from the Christian viewpoint of Meaningful Existence. This I achieved systematically by carrying out an analysis, interpretation and Christian evaluation of the philosophy as felt pulsating in every page of the four major novels under discussion.

The framework of the study, therefore, consists of the following, namely: THE INTRODUCTION; Chapter I – THE BACKGROUND OF THE STUDY; Chapter II – MEANINGFUL EXISTENCE FROM THE CHRISTIAN VIEWPOINT; Chapter III – THE HEMINGWAY WORLD, HIS CONCEPT OF LIFE, OF MORALITY AND OF THE NATURE OF MAN; Chapter IV – HEMINGWAY'S PHILOSOPHY OF MEANINGFUL EXISTENCE; Chapter V – HEMINGWAY'S PHILOSOPHY OF MEANINGFUL EXISTENCE AS REVEALED IN THE SUN ALSO RISES; Chapter VI – HEMINGWAY'S PHILOSOPHY OF MEANINGFUL EXISTENCE IN A FAREWELL TO ARMS; Chapter VII – HEMINGWAY'S PHILOSOPHY OF MEANINGFUL EXISTENCE IN FOR WHOM THE BELL TOLLS; Chapter VIII – HEMINGWAY'S PHILOSOPHY OF

MEANINGFUL EXISTENCE IN <u>THE OLD MAN AND THE SEA</u>; and Chapter IX – CONCLUSION.

The INTRODUCTION includes the definition of terms, the delimitation of the problem, and an acknowledgment of the author's gratitude. The vital terms to be defined are: CRITICAL STUDY, PHILOSOPHY, and MEANINGFUL EXISTENCE.

CRITICAL STUDY:

A critical study is an attempt to analyze, interpret, and evaluate anything. To understand this definition fully, let us break it down into its significant words. Analysis is the process of chopping down a whole, whether physical or abstract, into its component elements. It may be physical, qualitative, or logical. Interpretation is the process of explaining a matter, an idea or a situation in a particular way. Evaluation is the process of appraising or judging the value of a thing or situation based on certain standards. And, since this book undertakes a Christian evaluation of Hemingway's Philosophy of Meaningful Existence, the Philosophy is approached and gauged from a Christian angle.

PHILOSOPHY:

Philosophy is the study or science of the truths or principles underlying all knowledge and being (or reality). It may be natural, moral, or metaphysical.[1]

---

[1] C.L. Barnhart (ed. In chief), <u>The American College Dictionary</u> (New York: Random House, Inc., 1960), p. 810

MEANINGFUL EXISTENCE:

Existence means a continuance in being or life. That which is meaningful is that which is full of meaning; and meaning is that which is intended to be or is expressed or indicated.[1] Therefore, Meaningful Existence means the fullness of that which is intended of life or of the continuance in being. And since it is human meaningful existence with which we are concerned, it means the fullness of that which is intended for human life.

To establish a well-planned presentation of ideas, I have decided to start off with the Introduction that covers the definition of terms and the framework of the study. Then, the book progresses to Chapter 1 – The Background of the Study, which includes the Biography of Ernest Hemingway and the summaries of his four major novels, namely, The Sun Also Rises, A Farewell to Arms, For Whom the Bell Tolls, and The Old Man and the Sea.

After having achieved the necessary preparations which the Introduction and Chapter I have provided, the book shifts to Chapter II to discuss Meaningful Existence Viewed from the Christian Angle. I feel it important to present the Christian philosophy of Meaningful Existence prior to the presentation of the Hemingway philosophy. This sets the stage for the Hemingway precepts to be silhouetted against the background of the Christian precepts enabling the reader to see the Christian elements in Hemingway's philosophy.

---

[1] C.L. Barnhard (ed. In chief), The American College Dictionary (New York: Random House, Inc., 1960), p. 810

Chapter III deals with the Hemingway's World, His Concept of Life, of Morality, and of the Nature of Man. It is inevitable that this study treats these vital topics before the discussion of Hemingway's Philosophy of Meaningful Existence because it is against this background that Hemingway came to the formation of such philosophy of Meaningful Existence.

Chapter IV treats Hemingway's Philosophy of Meaningful Existence. This is an overall deduction from his four major novels.

Chapter V expounds Hemingway's Philosophy of Meaningful Existence as revealed in <u>The Sun Also Rises</u>. This is substantially a picking-up of vital points, through character delineation and situation analysis.

Chapter VI discusses Hemingway's Philosophy of Meaningful Existence in <u>A Farewell to Arms</u>. This receives the same treatment as the preceding chapter, but the material of analysis, interpretation, and evaluation involved is <u>A Farewell to Arms</u>.

Chapter VII elucidates Hemingway's Philosophy of Meaningful Existence in <u>For Whom the Bell Tolls</u>. It is practically treated in the same way that the two preceding chapters have been treated. However, the novel that occupies this chapter's concern is <u>For Whom the Bell Tolls</u>.

Chapter VIII explains Hemingway's Philosophy of Meaningful Existence in <u>The Old Man and the Sea</u>. This undergoes the same process as that which was undergone by the three previous chapters, except that this chapter deals with <u>The Old Man and the Sea</u>, which earned for Hemingway the Pulitzer Prize and the Nobel Prize for Literature in

1954.

Chapter IX, the CONCLUSION, undertakes the job of tying-up elements in the four major novels that substantiate Hemingway's Philosophy of Meaningful Existence. The objective behind this is to carry out a clear and well-systematized process of tracing the development of said philosophy from novel to novel. Moreover, as the critical study of any subject demands the technique of evaluation, I have chosen to work out a Christian evaluation of Hemingway's philosophy of Meaningful Existence.

As I had poured my thoughts and efforts into this work, its completion gives me a comforting joy. I am hopeful that, as the reader slips his finger through each page of this book, every page turned would give him an added knowledge that will enrich his moral vision and lead him toward a truly Christian way of life!

CHAPTER I
BACKGROUND OF THE STUDY

A Brief Biography of Ernest Hemingway[1]

Ernest Hemingway, the great American fiction writer, was born in Oak Park, Illinois, on July 21, 1898. His father, Clarence Edmonds Hemingway, was a doctor and was famous for his great skill in hunting and fishing. Ernest's mother was a singer in church; her deep religiosity coupled with her domineering nature rendered her incapable of understanding her husband. Consequently, although the family was well-respected in town, Ernest felt the lack of love in his home life. The superficial compatibility existing between his parents became the nucleus of his unhappiness in his boyhood.

Ambitious to pattern their son's life after theirs, Ernest's parents worked separately to infuse into his mind their respective interest: Ernest's mother exposed him to music, particularly church music, and bought him a cello; his father tended him towards hunting and fishing. At three, he bought him a rifle, and at ten, a fishing rod.

Ernest was the second of six children. He spent the summers in a wild and carefree way at the Walloon Lake in Michigan. He would go with his father on professional visits to an Indian camp back in the

---

[1] Most facts have been taken from the book entitled Hemingway and His Critics, edited by Carlos Baker and published in New York by the Hill and Wung Inc., in 1961; also, some information was derived from Charles Fenton's book entitled The Apprenticeship of Ernest Hemingway, published in New York by the Viking Press in 1954.

Michigan woods. Traces of his literary talents were first seen at school in Oak Park, Illinois when he became the editor of Trapeze, the school's weekly paper.

His early impressions of the loneliness of life which he derived from his experiences at home ripened into a belief that in life, one must be tough for only the strong and the tough ones survive. This belief in "survival of the fittest" was implanted in his mind by a series of experiences he had in school.

During his first lesson in Boxing at age fourteen, he sparred with a flabby middleweight, breaking his nose and losing his sight. In spite of the incident, he continued the course, and on the second day, to everyone's astonishment, he returned to the gym. At this age, he forced himself to face danger because he wanted to prove to himself that "he was not that scared."

Unfortunately, however, the impairment of his eyesight caused him to be rejected from service in the American army when America joined the war in 1917. So, after graduation from high school, he decided not to go to college. Instead, he went to Kansas City and worked as a cub reporter for the Star, one of the biggest newspapers in circulation in the Middle West. Here, he dealt particularly with local crimes and accidents.

In the spring of 1918, he enlisted himself as an ambulance driver in the American Red Cross. This job took him to the Italian front where he experienced real danger in war.

On July 8 of the same year, stationed at Fossalta di Piave, he was hit by fragments from an Austrian trench mortar bomb. He felt he died then. According to him, he felt that his soul got out of his body just like a silk handkerchief being pulled on one corner from a pocket. Then it turned around and got in again and he felt he was not dead anymore. Regaining consciousness, he found his two Italian companions dead, and one, legless and screaming.

He carried him on his back and walked towards the trenches; but, as he did so, two Austrian searchlights caught him in their beams, setting off machine gun fire that hit him in the knee and ankle. Nevertheless, he boldly went on with his burden until he reached a first-aid dugout where he collapsed. The soldier whom he tried to save was dead. The surgeons at the hospital where Hemingway was taken found two hundred thirty-seven steel fragments in his legs. Out of this number, only twenty-seven were removed. During his confinement, he was awarded the Croce de Guerra with three citations and the Medaglia d'Agenti al Valore Militare which was the second highest Italian Military decoration. Moreover, he was given a pension of about $50.00 a year.

With all these souvenirs of war, including the remaining metal fragments in his legs, an aluminum kneecap, and a grafted bone in his foot, he went back to Oak Park in the spring of 1919. From the occurrence of the deadly event, he suffered from insomnia. He could sleep during the day but at night he could not for fear that, in sleep, his soul might get out of his body and not come back anymore. This fear was echoed in one of his works when he said:

> I, myself, did not want to sleep because I had been living for a long time with the knowledge that if I ever shut my eyes in the dark and let myself go, my soul would go out of my body. I had been

blown up at night and felt it go out of me and go off and then come back. I tried never to think about it, but it has started to go since, in the nights just at the moment of going off to sleep; and I could only stop it by a very great effort.[1]

In 1920, he went to Chicago and met Sherwood Anderson and his friends. He also met Hadley Richardson with whom he fell in love and whom he married in September 1921.

After a brief honeymoon, he went to Toronto and landed a job at the Toronto Star where his short stories were published. In December, 1921, he was sent to Europe as a roving correspondent of the Toronto Star.

In Europe, he met Gertrude Stein through a letter of introduction given him by Sherwood Anderson. He also met Ezra Pound. He presented to Gertrude Stein his poems and the novel he was writing. The poems pleased her, but the novel did not, finding it excessively descriptive. She advised Hemingway to "begin all over again and concentrate."

For the Toronto Star, however, he was concerned with the Greco-Turkish War.

In November 1932, he went to Lausanne for a conference that dealt with the peace settlement between Greece and Turkey. His wife, Hadley, came to bring him his first manuscripts, consisting of a complete novel, eighteen stories and thirty poems. Unfortunately, the suitcase which contained all of these was stolen. However, this event

---

[1] Ernest Hemingway "Now I Lay Me," The Fifth Column and the First Forty-Nine Stories (New York: Random House), p. 461

did Hemingway some good for it forced him to follow Stein's advice.

In 1923, his Three Stories and Ten Poems was published by the Contact Publishing Company in France.

In 1924, In Our Time, his second booklet appeared. It consists of vignettes of post-war life intended to be inserted between the stories of In Our Time. In Our Time, published in New York in 1925, is Hemingway's book of stories. Financially speaking, this book was a failure.

In 1926, two of his works were published – the Torrents of Spring, his second American book, and The Sun Also Rises, which produced a sensational effect upon the people, especially among the young generation. The sale of the latter went as high as twenty-six thousand copies in the first year of its publication. Its force of influence was vividly seen when young boys and girls began to talk and act in the Hemingway manner. In March 1927, Hemingway broke off with Hadley Richardson. In the latter part of the same year, he married Pauline Pfeiffer, an editor of Vogue Magazine. The new couple stayed in Key West, Florida from 1928 to 1938 where Hemingway became known as a skilled fisherman and hunter.

In 1929, his war novel entitled A Farewell to Arms was published.

In 1923, Death in the Afternoon, his book on bullfighting, appeared.

In 1935, Green Hills of Africa, a book on his hunting expedition in Africa, was published.

The Civil War broke out in Spain in 1936. Hemingway acted to help Spain. He raised forty thousand dollars ($40,000) with which to buy ambulances for the loyalist armies. Unhesitatingly, he went to the place of war together with many other intellectuals who fought in defense of the Spanish Republican government. His experiences in this Civil War, coupled with what he had learned about Spain for eighteen years supplied him the materials for his novel, For Whom the Bell Tolls.

On November 4, 1940, just after the publication of For Whom the Bell Tolls, Pauline Pfeiffer divorced him. On November 21, Hemingway married Martha Gellhorn in Cheyenne, Wyoming.

In 1942, he gave his yacht, Pilar, to the United States Navy and volunteered to serve as a one-man suicide squadron. He cruised by himself off the North coast of Cuba with the aim of attracting the enemy submarines. His plan was to blow up any enemy submarine that may come along, and to blow himself up with it. He kept this mission from 1942 to 1944 but no enemy submarine came within hailing distance. His mission, however, enabled him to give vital information about the place where the German subs appeared. And had Hemingway not been called by the Naval attaché in Havana, he would have successfully carried out his plan because a German submarine appeared at the very spot which he had selected, twenty-four hours after he had been called into Havana.

In 1944, he joined the French Resistance Force and became the commanding general of a unit of irregulars.

After the Second World War, he wrote a short novel entitled Across the River and Into the Trees, a story of a bitter, aging colonel's lost love affair with a nineteen-year-old girl.

Hemingway's third marriage, just like the preceding ones, ended in divorce. His fourth wife, Mary Welsh, stayed with him until his death in 1961.

Hemingway and Mary Welsh settled at Finca Vigia (or Lookout Farm) near Havana. Here, Hemingway busied himself with writing and fishing. His fishing experiences here as well as those at Key West provided the necessary material for his novel, <u>The Old Man and the Sea</u>, which was published in 1952. This novel won for him the Nobel Prize for literature in 1954.

At <u>Finca Vigia,</u> he seemed to have had a fine and peaceful life. With his able wife, who could efficiently work on the family budget and income tax returns, they were able to live contentedly. Hemingway had a separate house for his three sons – John (or Bumby), Patrick (or Mousie), and Gregory (or Gigi). The royal household of the Hemingway's had a staff of servants who attended to the home necessities such as cleaning, cooking and gardening. In the afternoons, the cook, oftentimes, would not know how many people to include for supper because of the indefinite number of visitors that come to see Hemingway.

About 1954, a temporary world-wide shocking announcement was heralded – that of Hemingway's death in his hunting trip to Africa. His plane crashed in the Sudan jungle near the Nile – a habitat of man-eating animals. Hemingway, however, survived the accident and managed to reach home safely amid the astonishment of the people.

In November 1960, Hemingway began receiving treatment for hypertension at the Mayo Clinic in Rochester, Minnesota. He was discharged in January 1961, but he returned for further treatment in

April. He was discharged from the hospital five days prior to his death.

Hemingway was reported to have accidentally shot himself to death while cleaning his guns in preparation for hunting. He died July 1, 1961.[1]

SUMMARIES OF HEMINGWAY'S FOUR MAJOR NOVELS:

The Sun Also Rises

At the beginning of the novel, Jake Barnes, the American protagonist and narrator, presents Robert Cohn as a middleweight boxing champion of Princeton. Robert Cohn is a romantic, quite strikingly different from the set of sexual cripples that inhabit the novel. Robert Cohn has developed a feeling of insecurity because of his unhappy marriages. As Jake says of him "He had married on the rebound from his discovery that he had not been everything to his first wife."[2]

Robert Cohn is also a novelist but, in Jake's opinion, a very poor one. Later, Cohn's literary friend, Braddocks, and Frances Clyne, Cohn's mistress, were introduced, as well as the prostitute Georgette and the nymphomaniac Lady Brett Ashley, who was then waiting for the approval of her application for divorce to marry a certain Mike Campbell. Lady Brett Ashley is really in love with Jake Barnes; but because Jake was rendered impotent by a war-wound, he is not capable

---

[1] E.P. Patanne, "Ernest Hemingway," The Sunday Times Magazine. July 30, 1961, pp 13-14.
[2] Ernest Hemingway, The Sun Also Rises (New York: Charles Scribner's Sons, 1954), p. 8.

of satisfying her desires. Consequently, Jake feels deep anguish; however, he bears such feelings without complaint. In Chapter VII, the two lovers are introduced to an old veteran named Count Mippipopolous. Practically, Book I, which winds up in this chapter, portrays nothing eventful, as it merely presents the parade of moral cripples (except the Count) who aimlessly move along from place to place searching for fresh, empty sensations. However, the behavior of these characters fits this style for it accentuates the dull ache atmosphere and tacitly expresses the mood of disillusionment and aimlessness upon which the novel is built. Book I, therefore, the setting of which is in Paris, practically offers not much information except that Brett was intimated as having slept with Cohn at San Sebastian.

In Book II, Jake goes on a fishing trip to Burguete with Bill Gorton. There, he finds a life of tranquility, peace, and freedom from emotional tensions. But though they enjoy their stay in this idyllic place, they must leave to attend the big fiesta of San Fermin. So, they proceed to Pamplona to rejoin the group of Brett, Mike Campbell, and Robert Cohn once again. As a grand feature of the fiesta, there is a bullfighting event which is accentuated by the remarkable performance of Belmonte and Pedro Romero, a 19-year-old bullfighter who excels in integrity, discipline, courage, and craftsmanship. Prior to this grand day of Romero's performance in the bullring, he receives a serious physical injury in a fight with Robert Cohn. For the night before Romero's performance, Brett goes with him, and Robert Cohn finds them in Romero's room and Cohn almost massacres him. He is knocked down fifteen times and, every time he falls, he tries to stand up to fight Cohn. The fight results in Romero's moral victory, despite physical defeat. Cohn is morally broken and is reduced to a "whimpering child." Earlier too, Jake and Mike are knocked down by Cohn. The quarrels incurred by Cohn are due to his love for Lady Brett Ashley and to his inability to believe that his love affair with Brett at San Sebastian meant nothing at all to the woman. Finally, he realizes his folly and accepts the truth. The noise and violence that characterize the activities of the fiesta, therefore, correspond to the disorderliness and messiness of the lives and affairs of the expatriate group.

The Pamplona affair is characterized by messiness, noise, disorderliness, violence, and empty fun. To gain serenity and tranquility of mind, Jake feels the need to look for a peaceful place. This feeling comes upon him also because, somehow, he realizes his folly; so, in a fit of remorse, he wishes to redeem himself. Henceforth, he goes to San Sebastian to live peacefully. There he finds tranquility and mental alleviation in listening to band concerts, swimming, reading and walking around in the afternoon. However, his peaceful stay in this idyllic place is interrupted by a telegram sent by Brett asking him to see her in Madrid and help her out of trouble. He acquiesces to the demand of the message and sees Brett the following day in Hotel Montana. The two lovers converse and Brett tells him that she has sent Romero off because she does not want to ruin him. Consequently, she decides to go back to Mike Campbell. And as the lovers' taxicab is stopped by the policeman directing the traffic, Jake's disseverance from an old self and from Brett, implicitly achieves completion.

A Farewell to Arms

An American, Frederick Henry, enlists in the Italian Army. Seriously wounded at the Isonzo, north of Piave, he is hospitalized for a few weeks. This confinement opens the gateway to his love affair with an English nurse, Catherine Barkley. At first, his intentions, mainly springing from sensuous desires, are not altogether serious. This love affair, however, develops into real love. When Frederick Henry goes back to the war front, his outlook on things suffers a change. He feels emotionally uninvolved in the activities of the war. Though physically present, his mind lives in his own world with Catherine. This emotional detachment reaches its peak during the eventful Caporetto retreat when he abandons his army, thereby, completely severing himself from the war and its ideals.

To escape Police authorities, he jumps into a river, removes all the stars of his uniform, and manages to reach Milan where an old friend Simons gives him some clothes. In civilian clothes, he reaches Stresa where Catherine is and stays with her for some time.

One night, Henry learns from Emilio that he, Henry, will be arrested in the morning; wherefore Emilio helps the lovers flee in a boat to Switzerland that same night.

Eventually, they settle in the mountains outside of Montreux. When winter comes, its heavy rains drive them to Lausanne where Catherine delivers her first child three weeks hence. Much to Henry's consternation, Catherine dies with her baby by a Caesarian operation.

Henry walks in the rain from the hospital to face a life and a world of emptiness and despair!

For Whom the Bell Tolls

Robert Jordan, an American student of architecture, volunteers to fight for the loyalist's cause in the Spanish Civil War. What urges him to join the war is his belief in its social ideals as the cause of human liberation.

Given the mission to blow up a strategic bridge, he goes to the mountains near Segovia to solicit the aid of guerilla units headed by Pablo and El Sordo. If Jordan could accomplish his mission to blow up the bridge, the advance of the Loyalists would be facilitated.

During his three-day stay in the mountains, he meets Pablo, Pilar, Maria, El Sordo, Andres, and other bandits. Maria relates the cruelties of the Fascists, recounting how the Falangists raped her and killed her father, a Republican Mayor. This narration is, however, counterbalanced by Pilar's recountal of the massacre of the Fascists.

Jordan senses the failure of the forthcoming attack. Despite this, he goes on with his mission with full dedication to duty. On the day scheduled for the blowing up of the bridge, there occurs confusion among the Loyalist forces which paralyzes the Loyalist campaign. Robert Jordan, however, successfully accomplishes his mission. In the process, El Sordo and his band achieve a heroic death. Robert Jordan gets wounded in the leg, disabling him to escape. He, thus, urges his remaining companions including Maria to leave him and escape. To give his companions time to escape, he thinks of engaging the pursuing enemies himself. While waiting for the enemies, he ponders on the heroic death of his grandfather in the American Civil War. Such thoughts sustain him, and as he prepares himself to die, he suffers neither bitterness nor regret for he realizes the worth and wisdom of his sacrifice.

The Old Man and the Sea

Santiago, an old Cuban fisherman fishes the Gulf Stream for eighty-four days without a catch. For the first forty days, a boy named Manolin accompanies him. Somehow, Manolin is forbidden by his parents to go with the old man; hence, after the first forty days, Santiago fishes alone. On the eighty-fifth day, Santiago decides to go farther out to try his luck in the deep waters. At noon, he hooks a great marlin which steadily tows his skiff northwest. With skilled precision, Santiago maintains a steady pulse of control on the line as the noble fish keeps going in the same direction. Santiago pours onto his task all his intelligence and craftsmanship. He believes that this is what he is born for and, hence, "in doing it, he is not just 'doing' but realizing his 'being'!"[1]

In the afternoon of the eighty-sixth day, Santiago beholds the fish as it jumps out of the water in a scythe-like manner. Seeing the beauty of the fish, Santiago admires it.

The fish keeps a constant pull of the skiff and accordingly, Santiago keeps a steady hold of the line that joins them. Santiago maintains this constant hold despite a cramp that paralyzes his left hand. His struggle with the fish causes him much physical pain. On one occasion, a strong jerk on the line made by the fish causes him to fall,

---

[1] Earl Rovit, "The Structure of the Fiction," Ernest Hemingway (New Haven, Connecticut: Twayne Publishers, Inc., 1963), p. 86.

producing painful cuts on his back and left hand.

On the eighty-seventh day, the fish changes its course from northwest to east. It begins to swim with the current. It continues to struggle seemingly wanting to prove its nobility, and its endurance and courage in suffering. This incites in Santiago a feeling of reverence, brotherhood, and love for the noble fish.

At noon of the eighty-seventh day, the third day of Santiago's fight with the fish, the old man harpoons the great marlin, causing a stream of blood along the way. He hauls it to his skiff and sets himself for home.

An hour after, a great Mako shark bites into the flesh of the noble fish, thus increasing the flow of blood and, thereby, causing the coming of more sharks. He successfully kills the sharks, but it is of no avail because nothing remains of his loved "brother" but its skeleton.

With a very light load now, the skiff could travel swiftly. Reaching the shore, Santiago pulls his skiff onto the shore. He shoulders his mast, and silently drags his way home amid the concerned, anxious townspeople. Later, Manolin goes to his shack to bring him some coffee. The boy finds him asleep, lying with his face down, his arms stretched out and his palms up. When he awakes, the two fishing comrades plan for future fishing. Then, Santiago goes back to sleep to dream of lions playing on a golden beach.

CHAPTER II

MAN'S MEANINGFUL EXISTENCE VIEWED FROM THE CHRISTIAN ANGLE[1]

What is man created for? Why does he exist? These are indeed puzzling questions which confront everyone's mind – questions which the more contemplative thinker absorbedly ponders upon and which the layman feels indifferent to. Yet, these continually pulsate in each man's mind, sharply asserting themselves in moments of man's solitude; and when man entertains them with a deeper concern, he becomes engulfed by their profoundness, and he experiences anxiety and fear.

Could not man just have formed himself and have given life to himself without the interference of a Creator? Could the universe, with all its splendor and beauty, ever have formed itself into its perfect order and harmony? To say "yes" to these questions is generally a non-Christian or, at least a non-religious commitment! Christians believe that man could not have formed himself and infused life into himself. For, the perfect organization of his body parts – their order and interdependence – point out to a magnificent workmanship of one Creator. Man could not have thought of making an intellect for himself

---

[1] Most ideas, with the exception of those found in the discussion of the Passion and Crucifixion of Jesus Christ, which have received an original treatment, have been based on readings from the book authored by C. C. Martindale, entitled <u>Man and His Destiny</u>, published in New York by the Macmillan Company in 1928.

to be able to think, for the mere thought of such idea already points out to the functioning of an "already-made" intellect. If man creates his own intellect for this purpose, the functioning of the intellect, therefore, comes before its existence. This is a ridiculous idea!

Man is created after the image of God, the perfect Good and as such, man's greatest concern is to follow the path of God. Since God is the perfect Good, man, therefore, should follow the path of the "good" to be able to reach the perfect Good. But how can man identify the "good"? God created man, instilling into his very nature an affinity to good and an aversion from evil. God equipped him with intellect and will to enable him to know and see the true and the good. The intellect, therefore, discriminates the true and the good from the false and the evil.

The law of Christian life is two-fold: firstly, man must use his powers properly in the ways that God made them to be used; and secondly, man must do what is just and right to God, to himself and to others. This law of life embraces all of man's moral existence, imposing upon him certain duties which he must accomplish, and entitling each man to his rights which his fellowmen must respect. The good and the just always outline man's proper use of his powers. Hence, man's power of speech must not be used to cause evil, harm or injustice to himself, to others and to God; man's power of thinking should not be used as an instrument of sin. It is, thus, man's duty to take rein of the thoughts of his intellect, the desires of his will, the activities of his senses, and the movements of his body parts so that none of these powers may lead him to sin or to the neglect of his duties. The second phase of the law of life consists in man's duties to himself

– like self-control and self-preservation; to others – such as justice and charity; and to God – which is to know, love, worship and obey Him.

If man complies with the law of life which is also God's command and will, he would be able to maintain the good order and perfect harmony of the world that God had created for us. On the other hand, however, should man fail to follow this law, he would bring disorder and chaos to the world in general, and to human society in particular. It is, thus, necessary that society at large, and each man specifically, should endeavor to adhere to this law to ensure harmony, peace, and order in the world. In this way, man performs his duties as a social creature, and he profits out of such performance, too, for it paves the way to his perfection. Compliance with the law of life, therefore, carries a social and spiritual significance as it extends its effects to society, in general, and to the spiritual well-being of the individual, in particular.

Unfortunately, however, man cannot perfectly comply with the law of life. For, man's passions weaken his determination to follow the path of reason. His mistakes make him aware of his imperfections, giving him a feeling of insecurity. Instinctively feeling the innate desire to seek the true and the good which God had instilled into his nature, the consciousness of his imperfection fills him with an absorbing fear and anxiety. However, man should not despair for there is Christ to redeem him from sin. In a sacrificial and loving manner, God descended and assumed the form of man to work out the redemption of all mankind! This is the meaning of suffering in its purest, most unselfish, and most loving essence, touchingly portrayed in the Crucifixion. What a sacrifice, overpowering with the gentlest love, with pure unselfishness and unparalleled humility! Indeed, it reveals a welling spirit of love and humility for God, the Creator of all, the Omnipotent Lord and Master, to have come down and humble Himself to redeem man. God lived a man's life for man to model his ways after Him, for man to follow His footsteps and be guided in the Christian way of life. He lived as an embodiment of love, charity, humility, chastity, and wisdom.

The Lord's Passion is an uninterrupted series of agony and pain. Therefore, it could be taken as a dramatization of man's life of continuous suffering. The way Christ had taken His cross and had carried it patiently, humbly, and uncomplainingly is expressive of the way He wants man to take the little crosses of his life. Christ's cross may be seen as the load of sins of all mankind. Hence, the more sins, the heavier the load, and the greater is the suffering of Christ. The willful carrying of the cross, therefore, expresses that Christ willfully took upon His shoulder the burden of the sins of mankind. His falls under the heavy burden of the cross could be imaged as a metaphor of man's moral falls due to sin. Just as Christ received the painful lashes from the cruel executioners, so man receives the painful lashes of life's cruelties. As Christ arose from each fall, so He wants man to arise from where he has fallen to walk on until he reaches his goal. Christ's goal in this bitter Passion is the accomplishment of His mission in His life – the redemption of mankind – thus, giving eternal salvation to man whom He loves, and at the same time pleasing His heavenly Father. Man's goal in this life is to reach God, the Ultimate Good, thereby attaining perfect happiness.

Life lays its cruel hand of pain on all, irrespective of class and rank. It asserts its cruelty to the guilty as well as to the innocent. What an injustice to penalize the innocent! But the holy and innocent Christ joyfully took upon himself the penalty for the sins He had not committed to atone for the sins of man. What an infinitely kind heart He must have! What an unspeakable love for man must have suffused His heart! He could have miraculously escaped Crucifixion and because He was innocent, He could have denied acceptance of the cross. But because He loved man, He joyfully accepted the cross and went on His way to Calvary, patiently enduring His painful sufferings. There could only be one reason for this joyous acceptance of the cross; it was nothing else but a superabundance of love! Love ties up all woes and sufferings with joy. Love fills a person with an ardent desire to give, to serve. It propels man to a greater concern for the object of his love than his own, inspiring in him a willingness to serve and suffer for the object of his love. Pain comes to man when he is denied the chance to serve and to suffer for the love-object, for he is denied the feeling of joy which is bound up with such suffering. Christ loves man and the climax of His passion, the Crucifixion, is an undying emblem of His glorious love. His pain at Calvary essentially came from man's failure to feel His love and to reciprocate it with an equal love. Henceforth, when He agonized on the Cross, he cried out "I thirst". It was not the physical pain, nameless though it might be, which caused Him deepest anguish, for He had borne all His sufferings on His way to Calvary without any word of complaint. But on the Cross, He cried out "I thirst" for as He gazed around, He felt the scarcity of souls that could reciprocate the love He felt for man. He thirsted for more souls: He thirsted for love! It was this deepest anguish that drew out this agonizing cry from His lips. Having reached the end of the journey and the goal of His mission, Christ on the Cross, said, "It is consummated" meaning, His mission is accomplished. Even Christ, therefore, in His human life lived meaningfully for He had accomplished the purpose of His existence. And as Christ is the model of mankind, His having a definite goal and a definite purpose to achieve conveys that man, too, has a definite goal in the scheme of existence, and has a definite purpose to achieve. He intimates to man, therefore, that human existence has a definite plan to follow. He conveys to man that man has a purpose for existence and a purpose which he can accomplish.

To enable man to accomplish the purpose of his existence, God has endowed him with intellect and will to be able to know and to discriminate the true and the good from the false and the evil, thereby enabling him to choose that which is true and good. Moreover, God has infused into man's nature a desire for the good. However, though it becomes a natural tendency for man to desire the common good, so many factors cross his life causing his reason to become dull and perverted.

No man desires the evil. For, man is created by God to reach a state of perfection and happiness and man knows that happiness, a feeling of well-being, can only be derived from the good. Evil, per se, can never be desired by man for its own sake. The only reason why man commits an evil act is that he adjudges as good what is intrinsically evil, and as evil what is essentially good. This does not, however, provide an excuse for man's sinful acts; for, being a rational creature equipped with intellect and will, he is responsible for every act he executes. This accounts for the "tragedy of man", for even in a state of perverted reasoning, man could still go on with the sinful act, thereby submerging himself in its sinfulness and suffer its consequent punishment.

Man commits sin, not because of its evil essence, but because he perceives something good in it. For instance, masochists hurt themselves for, in doing so, they feel a peculiar sense of pleasure that satisfies them and makes them happy. The goal, therefore, is the attainment of happiness, which is by itself a good end. Moreover, one who commits suicide feels a greater good in ending his life than continuing a life of miseries. Man, therefore, always aspires for the good and seeks the greater good if choice is demanded, and further tends towards the greatest good if he recognizes it. It is, however, unfortunate of man if, in the process, his mind is in a state of perversion. But, as has been said, man should not despair for there is God to redeem him with the rest of mankind!

However, despite life's being portrayed as a chain of agonies and miseries, there is some joy bound up with its sufferings. Man should take life as a "glorious gift of a Loving Creator,"[1] for, through it, man is given the chance to earn worthily his state of perfection which gives him his subjective end of perfect happiness. Life, therefore, is a good which God has endowed upon him, and as such, man should preserve it and protect it from injury. However, man should not confine that spirit of life-preservation to himself alone but should be extended

---

[1] Vincent Martin, O.P., <u>Existentialism</u> (Washington 17, D.C.: The Thomist Press, 1962), p. 29.

to others as well. In other words, man should not take the life of another because, just as he has a right to life which he feels to be good and which deserves to be preserved, so do others have the same right. And that he must respect! Moreover, life could also be taken as a prayer which demands sincerity, fervor, and sacrifice. Every sacrifice in life, therefore, which may take the form of a suffering is graced with a spiritual joy since it carries with it a religious significance.

Finite things cannot quench the thirst of man. For man's thirst is infinite and, therefore, it demands something equal to it to be able to satisfy it. Man's thirst, thus, demands something which is also infinite. Pleasure gives man an evanescent happiness.

To live on pleasure alone, therefore, is a foolish enterprise because the happiness it gives is not enough to quench the infinite thirst of man. It does not give man the full satisfaction and perfect happiness he aspires for. If man should follow the path of Christ which will necessarily demand adherence to the law of life, he may attain his objective end, God, who will give him his ultimate subjective end, perfect happiness. Man must pass through a ladder of Christian principles, making the created goods – like the goods of the body, health, wealth, knowledge, food, material possessions, and others – as stepping stones to the attainment of the Greatest Good. Temporal pleasure, if it is sinless, is a form of good. However, it should not be given foremost concern as to sacrifice a greater good. It is not all there is in life. In fact, if it takes the sinful form, it becomes injurious to the health of both body and soul. Excessive pleasure tires man; yet renders him dissatisfied, thereby, inclining him to crave for more. The happiness that man derives from this as well as from all other created goods is transient, for there constantly hangs over him a cloud of threat that says, "everything lapses and soon!" Man should aspire for something which does not lapse, something infinite. Thus, he should seek God for it is only God, the Supreme and Greatest Good, which could fill in all of man's capacity for desire. God puts an end to man's craving for He satisfies all of man's desires. Attainment of the Ultimate Objective End, God, imparts to man the satisfaction of perfect happiness. Yes, perfect happiness – a state of complete freedom from all pain and evil, the satisfaction of all the good man desires, and a certainty that never shall he lose it. "God made man what he is in order that he may become perfect in his order or line and reach, thereby, his happiness and give the perfect glory to his Creator."[1]

If man attains this goal, he has accomplished his mission and has, therefore, achieved a meaningful existence. And so, with Christ at Calvary, he could say, "It is consummated," meaning "It has been accomplished." And only after this could man confidently breathe forth his soul to his Creator and express in the words of Jesus Christ – "Father, into Thy Hands, I commend my spirit!"

---

[1] C. C. Martindale, <u>Man and His Destiny</u> (New York: The McMillan Company, 1928), p. 51.

CHAPTER III
THE HEMINGWAY WORLD:
HIS CONCEPT OF LIFE, OF MORALITY AND OF THE NATURE OF MAN

The Hemingway world is conceived as a medium in which the life-giving air is saturated with death-like elements of doom. It is a world in which violence, chaos, and pain are set at a constant. Its forces cast their ghost-like shadows upon the lives of men, continually asserting their destructive hostility to all of mankind. Nothing in this world seems friendly. Everything takes on the figure of a contemptuous giant enemy, ever-cautiously watching and waiting for a chance to have a hard grip of man in order to smash him to pieces. Against these gigantic forces of destruction, man appears as a very tiny, helpless creature; and in a state of confusion, he wonders how and why he was cast into this world. He begins to question his identity and during his existence, he arrives at a self-realization through a discovery of truths about life. He discovers that life is schemed as a game wherein the cruelties and pains exist as a natural component.[1] He learns that he is thrown into the world to participate in the game of life; and as he goes on living from day to day, he learns the rules and the stakes of the game, and eventually, learns what life means. His experiences, thus provide him with such knowledge as will put him in a position to deduce his

---

[1] Earl Rovit, "The Code: A Revaluation," <u>Ernest Hemingway</u> (New Haven, Connecticut: Twayne Publishers, Inc. 1963), p. 109.

own values from which he could pattern out his life and by which he could react properly to the circumstances that life presents. In this way, thus, man creates his own values since the world in which he lives is devoid of all sense of value.

Hemingway has designed the game of life as a continuous strife which goes on its eternal process of complete annihilation of mankind. For man to preserve himself, he must learn the rules of the game adequately, speedily, and efficiently. He should endeavor to prove himself better than those who had already played it. Pitted helplessly against the cruel forces of the universe, he struggles valiantly; but such struggle is doomed from the start. He is, thus, viewed as a helpless creature placed inside a huge ball that continually rotates by itself to destroy him. Though he struggles courageously, eventually he dies. However, Hemingway gauges triumph not from the standpoint of whether one dies. What matters to him is whether death breaks him morally or disheartens him. Even with death, therefore, one can still gain triumph if he meets or faces it with full will and unbroken determination – stoically and courageously.

Hemingway portrays suffering as a test for man's dignity. It is taken as an inevitable component of life. Mental suffering consists in the foreknowledge of life's cruelties and of man's ultimate doom. Joy is not a positive entity but is a mere privation from suffering. The relief from suffering, momentary though it may be, serves as an interlude to man's continuous life of pain; thus, this gives him some feeling of rest, peace and relief. And where there are these elements present, man experiences a sense of joy.

As had been stated earlier, Hemingway believes that man must complete an action before he can discover its essence. Following this line of thought, therefore, one can rightly conclude that, to Hemingway, doing precedes being. This idea enervates Hemingway's concept of morality. To him, "what is moral is what you feel good after and what is immoral is what you feel bad after."[1] He, therefore, advocates that values are "a product and not a determinant of experience."[2] On account of this, the Hemingway man ventures to indulge in active living – inquisitive to find out how things are done and what it feels like to do them. Thus, a good act can only be discriminated from a bad one when the process of doing it has achieved some sort of completion. To Hemingway, the good is not what man wants to do, but it is that which gives man a feeling of well-being, of self-completion (wholeness) after action has been completed. This feeling of well-being may be attained through indulgence in or the sacrifice of immediate desires.[3]

To Hemingway, thus, the sense of the "good" is not a value that propels his people to action. It is not the cause, but rather the effect of action.

Hemingway's concept of morality, therefore, is nestled on the plane of sensation. He gives much emphasis on pleasure, which labels him as a supporter of hedonism. His concept of morality, which has been brought down to the low level of sensation portrays his belief in

---

[1] Ernest Hemingway, <u>Death in the Afternoon</u> (New York: Scribener's Sons, Inc., 1932), p. 4.
[2] Earl Rovit, "The Code, A Revaluation," <u>Ernest Hemingway</u> (New Haven, Connecticut: Twayne Publishers, Inc., 1963), p. 117.
[3] Ibid.

the impact of sensation upon man's consciousness. This fits all too well with the nature of his characters and the demands of his situations. His scenes are usually pasted against a background of war or its consequences. Can war, with all its exigencies, afford to give man time to contemplate on things calmly and deeply? Can man still soundly philosophize on matters and ponder on conventional morality with all the rush and cold bloodshed he witnesses? Man's life itself, in a situation such as this, is not completely his own; for any time, the indifferent noose of death may take it away from him! Man's tendency, therefore, is to live life as much as he can, and as the situation gives him not much time, he resorts to the gratification of his senses for it is on this plane alone that he can relish immediate satisfaction.

The presence of evil is not manifested in Hemingway's world in a concrete way. It is noteworthy to find no character in Hemingway's world who moves as an embodiment of evil per se. In other words, no character performs a bad act just purely because of its evil essence. At this point, thus, Hemingway bluntly implies that evil is a mere privation of the good;[1] hence, it does not appear in positive horrible forms in his world. In view of this, the Hemingway people move on a frontier of innocence despite the evil acts they perform. The purpose incorporated with the evil act committed masks its essence and elevates it to a level of dignity. Hence, there is dignity in Hemingway's thieves, whores, gamblers, and killers.

Hemingway divides his society or his people into two groups: those who are "one of us", the "have nots" who have been "there" in

---

[1] Earl Rovit, "The Code: A Revaluation," Ernest Hemingway (New Haven, Connecticut: Twayne Publishers, Inc., 1963), p. 122.

life's arena of struggles and those who are "not one of us" – the "haves" who have not been "there".[1] The first group "can be trusted in their self-trust"[2] and are, therefore, worthy to live in accordance with the rigorous measures of the Hemingway code, which we will discuss in the next chapter. The "have nots" are bare of material possessions and security. Hence, completely exposed to the pains of everyday living and struggle, they can understand what life really means and deduce from such experience their true values by which to live their lives properly and meaningfully. These "have nots" in Hemingway's terms, are the simple men – the bullfighters, the thieves, the soldiers – who, exposed to the trials of existence, are ripped of all false illusions.

The "haves" on the other hand, are those who are armed with comfort, security, wealth, and other material possessions that conceal from them the actual pains of life. Thus, they are full of illusions about life and about themselves and they live in too much indulgence. Because of their minimal exposure to the bare actualities of life, they fail to create realistic values that could guide them, since they have insufficient and artificially colored facts upon which to base such values. This group in Hemingway's world consists of the sophisticates, the intellectuals, bootleggers, and aristocrats – who live amid false illusions and who die with many illusions still in them. They, therefore, spend their lives aimlessly and meaninglessly without a true realization of the real essence of life. It is the "have nots" that discover the truths

---

[1] Earl Rovit, "The Code, A Revaluation," <u>Earnest Hemingway</u> (New Haven, Connecticut: Twayne Publishers, Inc., 1963). p. 122.
[2] Ibid.

about life and, thereby, find adequate means to live it meaningfully before it destroys them. They are the group of "awares" casting their silhouettes against the "unawares".

If one delves into man's psychological set-up, he will find that the psyche of man while in a state of turmoil and despair over human predicament either retracts to preserve itself or struggles to assert its superiority. If man's psyche retracts, he will tend toward isolation or indifference to the human situation. Nevertheless, in this state of his isolation, his psyche rebels silently, indignantly but helplessly. His would be a restrained rebellion devoid of violence and bloodshed; but such conditions place him in a burning pan of restlessness. He suffers inwardly and his tormenting helplessness drives him to a cold despair. He becomes restless and sleepless, continually brooding upon his state – his life which is meaningless. His life then will just be a resigned acceptance of his fate. On the other hand, however, should he choose to rebel actively to assert his superiority, his inhibited psyche, energetically impregnated by a burning disillusionment, comes in a crackling boom of violence. Thus, he takes a violent path of life. He struggles for his existence with a resolute determination to dominate the forces that crush him. But since his strength is not sufficient to subdue the world, his struggle is doomed. Nevertheless, his endurance to withstand life's pains, his competence and courage before life's trials save him from total loss and disillusionment. For beneath the apparent physical defeat lies a moral victory which is earned for him by his unbroken spirit. This victory enriches him with a greater moral power to face the brutalities of the graceless universe whereby, with a kept-up dignity, courage, and integrity, he achieves a meaningful existence.

CHAPTER IV
HEMINGWAY'S PHILOSOPHY OF MEANINGFUL EXISTENCE

Having discussed the nature of man and his situation in Hemingway's indifferent universe, we can now expound Hemingway's philosophy of Meaningful Existence.

With the world envisioned as one which seethes with violence, chaos and destruction, man comes into view, in his innocent inexperienced state. When life lashes on him its first cruel whip, man experiences a shock. As he experiences more, he learns what life means. He then becomes engrossed with learning the ways to preserve himself. Likewise, the Hemingway man undergoes a process of learning how to live life and, during this process, he eventually learns what life means. He, thus, builds up an edifice of rules to which he must adhere with discipline and resolution if he desires to remain morally whole. This set of rules embodies a code which the Hemingway hero embraces and respects. He creates a world of his own, shared by others who adopt and respect his code. This code consists of an active, valiant acceptance of the ills of life and the freedom from false illusions, living only by those which one's capabilities permit. Because courage and dignity are the only remaining values in this world, man should uphold them even through suffering or death. Therefore, under no circumstance must he give himself to a public display of emotion and suffering. He must elicit the least of emotion and must maintain that "grace under pressure." A spirit of stoicism and hard-boiledness, therefore, should characterize man's behavior before pain and death. If he endures with courage and unbroken spirit, he preserves his dignity; thus, he can keep "one small place clean and well-lighted" in his existential nature amid the dark, disorderly chaos of the universe in which he lives. In his existential nature, therefore, he can give room to meaning despite the pervasive darksome atmosphere of non-meaning which the outside world presents.

The Hemingway code is a set of rules that guide man in an active participation in life and enables him to accept the ills of life with courage and integrity. It embodies two vital lessons which the Hemingway hero must learn and relearn: first, the "ability to make realistic promises to oneself" and, second, the "ability to forgive oneself one's past."[1]

The code is likened to a bridge, one end of which is rooted to a past and the other leads to a future. It should be understood, however, that the past should not have a complete and rigid hold of man as to rip away from him his freedom at the present moment. The past should only serve as a reservoir of experiences which helps man meet the demands of the present moment with a sounder and more realistic attitude. Under no circumstance, therefore, should the past impose rigidly its influence upon man's present actions as may deprive him of his freedom of responsible choices. Hence, not pre-determined by his past but made richer by its effects on his emotional and mental set-up, man is able to make realistic promises to himself of what the future holds. It is necessary that man learns to forgive himself of all his

---

[1] Earl Rovit, "The Code: A Revaluation," <u>Ernest Hemingway</u> (New Haven, Connecticut: Twayne Publishers, Inc., 1963), p. 114.

imperfections and past inadequacies to be able to start anew. From the lessons he gains from his past experiences, he could improve himself; thus, face his future with a sounder, realistic knowledge of how to live life properly.

Consequently, the present convictions of man have somehow been molded by his past experiences and will, in turn, pattern out his future convictions. Nevertheless, it should be remembered that Hemingway emphasizes that man must not forget his past experiences but must be able to forgive himself his past imperfections – thus, "forgiving without forgetting" in Earl Rovit's phrase.

Life is a series of pitfalls wherein, with every fall of man, there comes a discovery of some truth, a realization of some imperfections. If this realization does not break him morally but instead prepares him for a sounder future way of life, then he emerges as a true Hemingway hero.

The code which the Hemingway hero and other members of his clan adopts, serves as a "cult" of discipline to impose some order in the disorderly, chaotic universe. Its rigorous measures call for rigid discipline. They call for physical courage and moral strength. They demand some rigid control of the emotion exploiting the capacity of man "to grin and bear."[1] So, if the Hemingway hero achieves success in following the code faithfully, he attains success in imposing some sense of order and meaning upon his existence.

It is, therefore, immaterial whether man's fate is doomed and

---

[1] Edmund Wilson, "Gauge of Morale," Ernest Hemingway: The Man and His Works, John K. M. McCaffery, ed. (Ohio: World Publishing Co. Inc. 1950), P. 241.

whether the world in which he lives seethes with total disillusionment and emptiness. What matters to the Hemingway figure is that he exists and that he must know the way to lead his life to make his existence meaningful. Since dignity and courage are but the remaining values in this world, it is given top priority by the Hemingway figure; he, therefore, aspires at preserving them at all costs for he believes that man's dignity, courage, and integrity depend upon his resources. As the Hemingway figure fights with dignity, courage, and integrity, he is given that moral wholeness that helps him achieve victory. There is a margin of victory in every defeat as there is a margin of hope in every disillusionment. Man, thus, should march onward in the battlefield of life, with a solid, steel-hard dignity and integrity, so that even as he falls dying, his unbroken spirit would still be able to assert its superiority, and in such defeat, achieve a moral victory! Then and there will he die happily, for, though he has been crushed physically, his inner core of manhood remains untouched, unbroken and whole continually asserting itself with dignity and integrity as the physical body droops and makes its final pose! As the Hemingway figure falls, therefore, his spirit arises to live in every heart and mind; for, seasoned by experience and unbroken by life's atrocities, he deserves the admiration of all mankind.

CHAPTER V

HEMINGWAY'S PHILOSOPHY OF MEANINGFUL EXISTENCE AS REFLECTED IN <u>THE SUN ALSO RISES</u>

<u>The Sun Also Rises</u> rests upon a mood of disillusionment. The nature of this disillusionment is one which has taken the form of a social habit. It portrays a generation wearied and demoralized by the war. These people move around the frontier of post-war life, searching for fresh sensations to be able to escape the memory of a past which they abhor. Most of the characters are morally impotent and they traverse the path of life aimlessly, satisfying the demands of their random impulses.

Only four of these people, strictly speaking, recognize the stakes in life, the real meaning of life, and what it takes to live meaningfully.

Following a hierarchical order of presentation of characters that have achieved meaningful existence – with reflections on the extent to which such characters have adhered to or fallen short of their created values and set rules of conduct and discipline with which they have made their existence meaningful – these characters march on to identify themselves as Jake Barnes, Bill Gorton, Pedro Romero, and Count Mippipopolous.

Jake Barnes, the narrator, and protagonist is plunged into a world of impossibilities. Rendered impotent by a war wound, he suffers much pain and despair. Paired with a nymphomaniac, Lady Brett Ashley, he suffers from emotional insecurity, for the nature of this woman with whom he is paired makes all sense of security in love relationship impossible. He is equipped with a rich capacity for desire to possess the woman he loves; but they are desires to which he could not sexually respond due to his war wound. As much as he desires to keep Brett in his room, he often fantasizes about staying in Brett's apartment. His desire only exacerbates his remorse and emotional pain. Although he undergoes an emotional crisis, he barely complains. He accepts his fate with stoical endurance. Juxtaposed with Cohn, a striking difference could be noted. Cohn shows a series of emotional displays – he proclaims his love for Lady Brett Ashley in public; follows Brett like a "sick bloody steer" when the woman is through with him; throws himself into disheartenment when Brett treats him like a perfect stranger after their brief affair at San Sebastian; and childishly cries when Romero breaks him morally during their fight. In contrast with Cohn, Jake Barnes moves within this circle with disciplined self-restraint in the face of life's pains. Despite his impotence, he bears it well, resentment and despair subdued without complaint. While he adheres strictly to the principles of stoicism in public, he fails to do so when alone with Brett. Thus, in one of his private conversations with Brett, Jake, in a state of long, suppressed emotional torture, bursts out into saying –

"Oh, Brett, I love you so much!"[1]

And later, he urges Brett, thus –

---

[1] Ernest Hemingway, <u>The Sun Also Rises</u> (New York: Charles Scribner's Sons, Inc., 1954), p. 54.

> "Couldn't we live together, Brett? Couldn't we just live together?"
>
> "I don't think so. I'd just tromper you with everybody. You couldn't stand it," replies Brett.
>
> "I stand it now."[1]

Notwithstanding this occasionally uncontrollable fall into sentimentality, there follows an immediate check-up of behavior, consciously laid out by Brett in compliance with a code of stoicism which she and the other members of the clique also adopt and share with Jake. Thus – when Jake brings out his emotions to Brett in the above quoted passages, concluding it with "You know I love you," Brett arrests his sentimentality promptly, saying "let's not talk. Talking is all bilge. I'm going away from you, and Michael's coming back."

If we are to probe into a deeper analysis of the manner of speaking and acting which the members of the clique adopt, it could be sensed that they are striving to forget an irreparable past which places them on the fringe of total moral breakdown. To achieve this objective, they must form an iron code of behavioral discipline, a sense of hardboiledness or stoical attitude toward all pains. Therefore, to maintain a "stiff upper lip" in the face of torture was, to them, of greatest and vital importance. In view of this, they abhor all people who tend to thwart their adherence to this rule. They abhor Cohn for the display of his emotions because it revives in them a deep-seated

---

[1] Ernest Hemingway. The Sun Also Rises (New York: Charles Scribner's Sons, Inc., 1954), p. 55.

emotional torture sealed beneath the adopted code of discipline that they have laid upon such emotions to be able to subdue them. A proof of an all-too-deep misery from which they suffer is vaguely insinuated in the following lines, while Jake and Brett dance together –

"Oh, darling," Brett said, "I'm so miserable."

I had that feeling of going through something that has all happened before.

"You were happy a minute ago."

The drummer shouted: "You can't two-time—"

"It's all gone."

"What's the matter?"

"I don't know. I just feel terribly."

". . .." the drummer chanted. Then turned to his sticks. "Want to go?"

"I had the feeling as in a nightmare of it all being something repeated, something I had been through and that now I must go through again.[1]

And at the end of the scene, they bade each other good night –

"Good night, Brett," I said. "I'm sorry you feel rotten."

"Good night, Jake. Good night, darling. I won't

---

[1] Ernest Hemingway, The Sun Also Rises (New York: Charles Scribner's Sons, 1954), p. 64.

see you again."

We kissed standing at the door.

She pushed me away. We kissed again.

"Oh, don't!" Brett said.

She turned quickly and went into the hotel…[1]

From the above passages, what appear conspicuous are: the assertion of a troubled but subdued emotion which renders the lovers restless, and the strict effort of these lovers to avoid any stimulus which may thin the layer of stoic discipline which they have laid over such emotion to suppress it. Moreover, it could be noted that once Jake's emotions are provoked, his threshold for sentimentality suffers a reduction; hence, he falls back into the memory of a painful past – "I had a feeling…" so he relates, "as in a nightmare of it all being something repeated, something I had been through and that now I must go through again." So, Jake and the other members of the clique avoid and abhor every stimulus that stirs the emotion. They abhor Cohn, most especially, for he stands as the external embodiment of their vague tormented emotions so much that the mere sight of him brings them to their painful past and back to an awareness of their emotional status. To make this point clearer, let us cite another instance in the novel. Jake and Brett comments on the romantic and sentimental behavior of Cohn:

---

[1] Ernest Hemingway, The Sun Also Rises (New York: Charles Scribner's Sons, Inc., 1954), p. 65.

"He depresses me so." (says Brett)

"He's behaved very badly."

"Damned badly. He had a chance to behave so well."

"He's probably waiting just outside the door now."

"Yes, he would. You know, I do know how he feels. He can't believe it didn't mean anything."

"I know."

"Nobody would act as badly. Oh, I'm so sick of the whole thing…"[1]

And later on, Jake relates – Brett was nervous as I had never seen her before.

She kept looking away from me and looking ahead at the wall.

"Want to go for a walk?"

"Yes, come on."

I corked up the Fundador bottle and gave it to the bartender.

"Let's have one more drink of that," Brett said.

"My nerves are rotten."[2]

---

[1] Ernest Hemingway, <u>The Sun Also Rises</u> (New York: Charles Scribner's Sons, 1954), p. 181.
[2] Ibid.

Mark that while in a state of emotional distress, they resort to drinking.

The novel floods with drinking. For, in the character's effort to forget the past, they find drinking indispensable. Since drinking is used to accomplish an essential objective, it is, thus, raised from a simple relish of sensation to a level of discipline. They must drink to gain momentary relief from the continuous and ever-persistent awareness of the pains of life. Jake's situation propels him to be in constant search for values. He views the world as a "good place to buy in," taking all things in life from the plane of simple exchange of values.

> "I thought I had paid for everything.
> Not like the woman pays and pays and pays. No idea of retribution or punishment. Just exchange of values. You gave up something and got something else. Or you worked for something. You paid some way for everything that was any good. I paid my way into enough things that I like, so that I had a good time. Either you paid by learning about them, or by experience, or by money.
>
> Enjoying living was learning to get your money's worth and when you had it.
>
> You could get your money's worth. The world was a good place to buy in."[1]

Thus, in a world which is stripped of practically all moral values, Jake creates and figures out his own norm of values. As he goes on living, he is in a continuous process of learning facts about life and

---

[1] Ernest Hemingway, The Sun Also Rises (New York: Charles Scribner's Sons, 1954), p. 148.

so he becomes deeply engrossed with learning "how to live in it." With every experience he undergoes, he achieves a self-realization and discovery of certain truths; hence, from the knowledge he acquires from these experiences, aided by his introspective nature, he can deduce his own sense of values from which to pattern out a meaningful existence. So, he says –

> ". . . Perhaps as you went along you did learn something.
> I did not care what it was all about.
> All I wanted to know was how to live in it.
> May be if you found out how to live in it you learn from what it was all about."[1]

Hence, in the early part of the novel, during the Paris episodes, Jake was still a novice, a "greenhorn" in the game of life. He was still in the first stage of the learning process. From his experiences in Paris, he realizes that he lives within a dull-ache atmosphere. His emotional wound is constantly and frequently punctured so that it cannot go on its continuous healing process. Thus, he searches for a healthier atmosphere. He goes on a fishing trip to Burguete with Bill Gorton; and there, with the healthful environment and activity, he, though an insomniac in Paris, can sleep with tranquility and freedom from emotional tensions.

Sports occupy a high position in the scheme of Jake's values. He gives it a higher regard than love – perhaps, as part of his healing techniques of rationalization because, for him, love is impossible. He subtly shows this higher regard through his position as narrator. While

---

[1] Ernest Hemingway, <u>The Sun Also Rises</u> (New York: Charles Scribner's Sons, Inc., 1954), p. 148.

resting and waiting for Bill's coming, he reads a book by A.E.W. Mason.

> The book was something by A.E.W. Mason, and I was reading a wonderful story about a man who had been frozen in the Alps and then fallen into a glacier and disappeared, and his bride was going to wait twenty-four years exactly for his body to come out on the moraine, while her true love waited too, and they were still waiting when Bill came up.
>
> "Get any?" he asked. He has his rod and his bag and his net all in one hand, and he was sweating. I hadn't heard him come up because of the noise from the dam.
>
> "Six, what did you get?"
>
> Bill sat down, opened up his bag, laid a big trout on the grass. He took out three more, each one a little larger than the last, and laid them side by side in the shade from the tree. His face was sweaty and happy.[1]

Juxtaposed with love, the thrill and happiness derived from sports (fishing) are laid in sharp contrast with the naked disenchantment, hopelessness and sadness which love brings. The presented idea that they (the bride and her true love) were still waiting hopelessly when Bill came up "sweaty and happy," betrays a hidden ironic sneer that Jake intends for love. Moreover, the portrayal of Bill as "sweaty and happy," the expected healthfulness of fishing as an exercise, and the natural healthfulness which the environment provides

---

[1] Ernest Hemingway, The Sun Also Rises (New York: Charles Scribner's Sons, 1954), p. 120.

– all of these bear overtones of good health. And the juxtaposition of the two situations – the possible falling of the bride's health due to despair, and the hopelessness and defeat she suffers from, as contrasted against the happiness and sense of triumph which Bill Gorton achieves, understates more clearly Jake's greater faith in sport as a means of help for the completion of the healing process which he undergoes. The futility of the bride's effort to wait for twenty-four solid years provides a magnificent metaphor of the futility of Jake's efforts in love. To the bride, as to Jake, love is impossible. If after twenty-four years of tedious waiting, the bride could see her lover – alive, then, the effort receives a worthy compensation. But in this case, the effort is in vain; for the only thing she could profit out of such sacrificial waiting, is the sight of her lover – dead! Though she sees her lover in compensation for her efforts, love is still impossible. Just as, although Jake sees his lover Brett and disregards his impotency, she is simply a plain physicality, for her emotional death disables her to respond to love as a normal woman!

Realizing that the tranquility and mental alleviation provided for by the healthful Burguete atmosphere, coupled with the joy and delight derived from fishing, are still insufficient to make Jake feel the real essence of meaningful existence, he, thus, goes to Pamplona to witness bullfighting in the San Fermin fiesta.

Bullfighting as Jake conceives it is the only sport which stands as a ritual of life. It occupies the highest position in his scheme of values because to him, it portrays a life in a world complete and independent of all the chaos and disorderliness which characterize the vast world in which he lives. He feels it as a portrayal of life because it enfolds the vital elements – the risk, grace, danger, and death. However, it shows its superiority over the actual life in which Jake lives because its details are carried out in an orderly fashion, unlike the disorderliness and pointlessness upon which actual life itself rests. In bullfighting, there is nothing unreasonable for the player of the game, the bullfighter, is held answerable to every happening in it. There are no surprises either, for the bullfighter has a full knowledge of the consequences of every move he makes. Tragedy which pervades the air with the ominous scent of death, is turned to an impossibility only if the matador rips away all fear, ignorance and gracelessness. Skilled and disciplined enough as to be able to follow the rules of the game, the matador moves along this frontier of trials and dangers with a maximum observance of "purity of line" and "grace under pressure." He performs with craft, intelligence, and courage.

Bullfighting is a controlled ordering of the vital elements of life. It portrays concretely the brutalities in life in the bloody killing that inevitably takes place in every game. It dramatizes man's violent struggle against nature embodied by the bull, and if the bullfighter is armed with skill, courage, integrity, and discipline, he conquers the bull by administering death on him. Likewise, if man, in his violent struggle against Nature, proves himself as a skillful, courageous, honorable, and disciplined player of the game of life, he achieves a conquest of Nature. However, if the matador falls short of all sense of integrity, skill and courage, the pendulum of tragedy that has been constantly hanging over him, waiting for a chance to get loose from its suspension, drops on him to administer his death or moral breakdown. In contrast with Jake who is still in the process of learning the stakes of the game of life, the matador, therefore, knows the stakes of the game he is playing beforehand – before his actual participation starts. He knows, as Jake would learn as he goes on living, the stakes of the game they play. In both games, bullfighting being a mere drama of life itself, manliness and self-respect are always held at stake and moral wholeness and victory depend on man's own resources.

In bullfighting, the matador faces a risk of death. An impending death constantly hovers over him. In view of this and of the courage with which he faces such danger, the matador lends moral seriousness to his actual life which lacks it. As he exists in a postwar world of moral decadence, he lives life fully and meaningfully in his own world of bullfighting; for, in it, there is a moral seriousness, discipline, integrity and a sense of order – elements which are found either absent or wanting in the world of actual living. As the matador exposes himself to violent risks, he experiences a thrill and with every successful, pure, and graceful move he makes, he experiences an elation. The greater risk he indulges in, the greater is the feeling of success and thrill and so he enjoys life more fully; for the gusto of living depends on the maximum exhilaration derived from a maximum exposure.

It has been mentioned earlier that in bullfighting, there is nothing unreasonable, for everything is within the control of the bullfighter and is dependent upon his capabilities. Everything stands resultant of every move he makes.

In this way, therefore, he assumes complete responsibility for his fate. Every wound, either moral or physical which he may incur in the game, is a consequence of a form of shortcoming on his part, deservedly received out of some inconsistency in his skill, discipline and craft. Compared with the game of life which Jake plays, it strikes a chord of contrast with the life-game. For, while the matador suffers no unreasonable wound, Jake suffers a wound, not of his own making, but that of the indifferent world. He, together with the other victims of the war, was hit by war's deadly fragments, either physically or morally, driving them to a despair which is not of their own making, but which the world had indifferently given them – without purpose, reason, or intention. The war wound received by Jake is, therefore, an unreasonable wound which has forced him into the position of a helpless, innocent victim, fated, without chance for choice, to accept all things done to him. This wound, which consequently causes Jake's impotence, throws him into the pit of sexual isolation, disabling him from living a complete life. Notwithstanding this, Jake is equipped with a great capacity of desiring to possess the woman he loves; his impotence, therefore, provides a perfect block to the fulfillment of his desires. This aggravates his emotional tensions and gives him deeper anguish. His inner world, therefore, is as confused as the outside world in which he lives. Consequently, his inner torment becomes compounded by the outside chaos and disorderliness he experiences, building up an edifice of emotional crisis.

In his brief stay in Burguete, it is noteworthy to find him experiencing some degree of mental alleviation, while separated from Brett. Through the healthful atmosphere, coupled with the enjoyment derived from fishing and male camaraderie, he feels relaxed and released from emotional tensions and is even able to sleep – something which he is unable to achieve while with Brett in Paris. This gives one an inkling of the solution to Jake's problem of knowing how to live life properly and how to make his existence meaningful. However, this solution, at this part of the story, takes on a very vague revelation and will only be felt to appear more sharply as Jake goes on living, until it uncovers itself completely before the close of the story.

This solution reiterates itself once more, and this time more sharply, when Jake goes to San Sebastian to redeem himself from his lost dignity in Pamplona.

In Pamplona, Jake allows himself to act as a go-between in Brett's seduction of Romero, thus, losing completely Montoya's high regard of and respect for him. Montoya, as well as Jake, knows everything that Romero represents. He represents discipline, integrity, and manliness – qualities which are found lacking in Jake and his friends; in view of this, he offers Jake and his friends a vicarious redemption. To Jake, therefore, he embodies the hope of the lost generation. Through the art of bullfighting, Romero achieves a proper ordering of the details of life, for every phase of it is placed under his control. Unlike the aimless members of the lost generation, he has a definite goal in life and, therefore, occupies a definite place in the scheme of existence. For this reason, Jake comments that it is only the bullfighter who lives life meaningfully.[1]

Having a full knowledge of Romero's qualities and value, Jake feels conscious of the great gap that separates the expatriates' world from that of Romero's; and he, with Montoya, realizes that these two

---

[1] Ernest Hemingway, The Sun Also Rises (New York: Charles Scribner's Sons, 1954), p. 148.

worlds should remain separate if bullfighting and the world it represents, should stay ever true and honest.[1] Despite these knowledge and realization, he gives in to Brett's desire for him to bridge the gap that separates these two worlds. He, thus, allows himself to become an accomplice in the liaison between Brett and Romero. By this act, he loses his self-respect and integrity, for his principles and powers of manly determination stand servitors to the caprices of woman. However, he realizes his folly and, in a fit of remorse, he decides to go to San Sebastian to start redeeming himself. He stays for some time in San Sebastian relaxing his mind through listening to band concerts and through swimming. His bath in the beach and his clean and deep dives into the water may stand emblematic of the cleansing process which he undergoes to rip away all the damages he had incurred in Paris.

However, his free and easy stay in San Sebastian, just like his idyllic stay in Burguete, has to be altered again by the interference of woman. For, soon he receives a message from Brett, saying –

COULD YOU COME HOTEL MONTANA MADRID AM RATHER IN TROUBLE BRETT

To which he replies –

LADY ASHLEY HOTEL MONTANA MADRID ARRIVING SUD EXPRESS TOMORROW

After this, Jake, himself, makes a sarcastic comment on his act, saying –

That was it. Send a girl off with one man. Introduce her to

---

[1] Melvin Backman, "Hemingway: The Matador and the Crucified," Modern American Fiction, A. Walton Litz, Ed. (New York: Oxford University Press, 1963), p. 204.

another to go off with him. Now go and bring her back. And sign the wire with love. That was it all right.[1]

In the above passages, therefore, it is made clear that Jake is even conscious of his folly; despite such consciousness, however, he wills to sacrifice his principles, dignity, and manhood on behalf of the woman he loves. His manhood, therefore, is one which is not independent of woman. When we come to the delineation of Romero's character, a clear-cut distinction between Romero's manhood and that of Jake's will be shown.

The atmosphere and mood of San Sebastian and Burguete show a vivid contrast with those of Pamplona. In the former, there is peace, serenity, and tranquility; there is freedom from mental and emotional stress; there is no tension produced by random activities. In brief, they are idyllic places where the mind can freely linger in peace. The latter is characterized by random activities, messiness, troubles, tension, noise and meaningless fun. These are all placed in the milieu of the San Fermin fiesta. Lady Brett Ashley may be pointed out as a personification of this as she is presented with a white garlic wreath around her neck, surrounded by a group of Riau Riau dancers. She and the fiesta stand symbolic of the meaninglessness that strikes a dominant key in the novel.

The fiesta gives a panoramic portrayal of meaninglessness since it is incorporated with the senseless, empty enjoyment in which the partakers drown themselves. Its tone of absurdity becomes sharpened by Vicente Girones' death while participating in the fun of

---

[1] Ernest Hemingway, The Sun Also Rises (New York: Charles Scribner's Sons, 1954), p. 148.

the fiesta. Vicente Gerones is a 28-year-old lad from near Tafalla who had started coming yearly to the fiesta from the time he got married. He was gored by a bull in the runway leading to the bullring as he joined the crowd of runners. The incident robbed his wife and two children of his fatherly tendance, protection, and support. Weighing both sides – the empty, senseless enjoyment derived from such meaningless participation on one hand, and the factors held at stake in such participation, on the other - one feels the absurdity of the idea of choosing to participate at the threat of losing those which are held at stake. And this scene is nothing else but a portrayal of just this absurdity. This absurdity and meaninglessness are subtly handled in the following passages:

> "You hear? Muerto. Dead. He's dead. With a horn through him. All for morning fun. Es muy flamenco" (said the waiter) "It's bad." "Not for me," the waiter said. "No fun in that for me."[1]

Here, Hemingway gives an adequate comment on the senselessness of the venture; and the death of Vicente Girones and its consequences render sharply and nakedly the very absurdity and pointlessness which such venture embodies. This silly enjoyment which Vicente Girones and the other participants of the fiesta embrace at the risk of essential stakes gives an illusion of true happiness which masks the very absurdity which lies in its inner core. Also, this gives a comment on the general behavior and mood that prevails in the period, particularly, among the members of the lost generation. These people

---

[1] Ernest Hemingway, <u>The Sun Also Rises</u> (New York: Charles Scribner's Sons, 1954), p. 198.

continually remain, or choose to remain, in ignorance about the proper way of living life, for the moral crimes they have undergone had caused them to lose practically all sense of values. This loss gives them a death-in-life—a moral death, and Vicente Girones is the physical representation of this moral death. Moreover, their inability to respond humanely to the incident uncovers the extent of their moral deaths. This is expressive of the moral condition of the time. This is the social ailment of the twenties.

On the other hand, Lady Ashley stands as a concrete figure of meaninglessness. She embodies meaninglessness because her path of life leads nowhere. Her existence does not lead to any definite goal. She has no purpose to achieve; she goes about aimlessly following the unpredictable path of the wind and the call of her random impulses. Even to Jake, she is a senseless illusion for she is something which Jake can never attain. The continuance of Jake's relationship with her is a futile gesture, an empty illusion from which Jake must free himself if he wishes to avoid the high possibility of mental imbalance.

Jake's stay in San Sebastian spending his time in reading, healthful swimming, walking, and listening to band concerts is to become a prelude to his final decision of self-abnegation. For, the contrast between the idyllic pleasures and the mental alleviation he had enjoyed in San Sebastian and Burguete, and the misery he has suffered in Pamplona with Brett was so stark that such experiences enabled him to reach the completion of his self-realization. He was able to detach himself from both experiences and look at each of them objectively. Brett is the personification of the fiesta – repressing the senseless activities and empty enjoyments of its partakers, tinged with self-deception and illusion that conceal the meaninglessness and absurdities of their lives. Jake's momentary separation from the fiesta, socially, and from Brett, personally, allows him to reflect on himself; wherefore, he marks a distinction between himself attached to such illusions and himself detached from such illusions. Thus, he comes to a self-realization, and he discovers and learns that to be able to live life properly and meaningfully, he should detach himself from any form of illusion. Since Brett is an illusion to him, being something, he can never attain, he should confront such illusion honestly and realistically and sever himself completely from it.

This he achieves in San Sebastian and Burguete, for which reason he finds peace, tranquility, and freedom from emotional tension. Earlier, before reaching this stage of Jake's self-realization and self-renunciation, Jake could not reconcile himself with reality. He insistently hoped that someday Brett and he would become a happy pair. He sensed the futility of this hope somehow, but his inability to accept reality drove him to bitter despair. He felt emotionally confused and physically helpless. But these experiences have widened up his vision about life and, though his days were saturated with pain, each day was impregnated with knowledge about life, so each was a day of mental achievement. Gradually, he learns to resign himself to reality; he learns to accept that the continuance of his relationship with Brett is an empty effort, for she is a futile unattainable illusion. He reaches this peak of the learning process in San Sebastian after having undergone painful experiences in Pamplona. The Hemingway code demands forgiving, without forgetting, past mistakes because it is the lessons in the past that draws out the path leading to the future. Thus, Jake forgives himself his past imperfections and arises to redeem himself and regain his lost integrity. He now makes his first decisive steps along a life-path of complete detachment from impossible illusions, living only by those which his capacities permit. Consequently, when he goes to Madrid to see Brett, the emotional distance between the two is conspicuously marked. His replies to Brett's remarks are tinged with irony and restraint, handled with a calculated pulse to shield his detachment. They almost never talked about their own love affair and when at the last portion Brett tries to draw his attention to it, he adequately shields his emotions from being reawakened by an air of irony and self-detachment. Hence, to Brett's statement of reproach "Oh Jake, we could have such a damned good time together,"[1] Jake replies "Yes, isn't it pretty to think so?"[2] This reply subtly expresses an emotional detachment since it is a cold, ironic reply. Furthermore, from the tenor of this reply, Jake is delicately felt in his present detached position, making an objective reflection on a past, old self. At this part, his detachment from false impossible illusions represented by Brett achieves completion, symbolically portrayed by the policeman who raises his baton to stop the continuance of the trip of the lovers. The pose of authority shown by the policeman is a pictorial representation of the order that Jake's new, discovered "self" imposes upon his old "self" to live only by those passions which his capabilities permit. He, therefore, should have a full knowledge of himself and should learn to acknowledge his limitations so that his passions and desires will not go

---

[1] Ernest Hemingway, The Sun Also Rises (New York: Charles Scribner's Sons, 1926), p. 246.
[2] Ibid.

beyond what his capacities permit.

Going a step higher in the hierarchical order of gradation of values, we have Pedro Romero, the young bullfighter. Pedro Romero is the embodiment of integrity, discipline, and independent manhood. Although Jake recognizes and shares his principles, Jake lacks the discipline and manly integrity which outlines Romero's personality. For this reason, before Jake's mind, Romero exists as a model and as a concrete embodiment of the principles which he respects but with which he is incapable of coping.

Romero's inner core of manhood had been formed and made hard by his real exposure to the elemental truths of life which he met in the bullring. His maleness is constantly pitted against the brutalities of Nature which has taken the form of the bull.[1] The risk of death to which he exposes himself – his life and everything he embodies – imparts moral seriousness to his task, and the courage with which he meets such risk graces him with a sense of dignity for which the post-war people thirst. Therefore, to those people in general who understand his principles and see and recognize his value and the qualities he embodies, and to Jake in particular, Romero offers the hope of vicarious redemption. To these people, therefore, Romero occupies a morally vital place in their hearts; and in the seduction of Romero by Brett, the expected outcome of which is Romero's destruction, Brett carries away all their hopes for vicarious redemption. Jake knew what it meant when he took part in facilitating Romero's seduction.

---

[1] Melvin Backman, "Hemingway: The Matador and the Crucified," <u>Modern American Fiction</u>, A. Walton Litz, Ed. (New York: Oxford University Press, 1963), p. 204.

However, this knowledge and Jake's principles taken altogether were not strong enough to incite in Jake a manly determination to command his will to follow his own principles. And weakened by emotional instability essentially caused by his physical and moral stand, he succumbs to the dictates of his emotion, sacrificing his integrity and manliness. It is at this point that he loses hold of his principles, and he makes a grave moral fall.

This fall is defined when Montoya loses his respect for Jake and implicitly shows that Jake is no longer "one of us." Jake's inability to divert himself from the senseless emotional path which is destructive to his manliness and self-respect leads him to great loss. For, by such actions he becomes guilty of self-deception, forcibly pushing his principles to the rear, consciously but devoid of manliness, giving way to empty emotionality. Thus, he loses touch of his principles; he loses his manliness and integrity - values which he should not lose at all costs.

The delineation of the nature of Jake's manhood uncovers a sharp contrast between Jake's manhood and Romero's. While Jake pays tribute to Lady Brett Ashley at the sacrifice of his dignity, Romero does it with no moral loss. To Romero, such undertaking is something independent of his integrity and manhood. Thus —

> Pedro Romero had the greatness. He loved bullfighting, and I think he loved bulls, and I think he loved Brett. Everything of which he could control the locality he did in front of her all that afternoon. Never once did he look up. He made it stronger that way, and he did it for himself, too, as well as for her. Because he did not look up to ask if it pleased, he did it all for

himself inside; and it strengthened him, and yet he did it for her, too. But he did not do it for her at any loss to himself. He gained by it all through that afternoon.[1]

As Pedro Romero performs in the ring, he is engaged in the vital elements of life – with grace, he takes the risk of danger and death although these elements are presented in an orderly fashion. Because he works with full sincerity, devotion, and dedication, he pours into his work all his intelligence, his discipline, his courage, integrity, and craft – thus, he instills in his work practically the whole of his being. And this solidifies his manhood, giving him that composure and confidence of spirit as he faces his opponent, the bull, a living entity of Nature, presenting before his eyes as it gallops to attack him, the brutalities of life.

However, Romero, skilled as he is, approaches him with dignity and proves his manly superiority over Nature as he proves his dominant control over all things. He moves along this frontier of life's struggles with no contortions but with that "old purity of line" and "grace under pressure" eliciting no unnecessary display of danger though he gives himself to a maximum exposure to it. Because Romero gives the whole of himself in the performance of his craft, he, thus, intimates the whole of his manhood with Nature. And it is this exposure of his manhood to the elemental forces of nature that develops it so that every fight he makes is a widening of experience and nourishment to his manhood. For, every fight means a new challenge to his manhood

---

[1] Ernest Hemingway, The Sun Also Rises (New York: Charles Scribner's Sons, 1954), p. 216.

which, with the new risk it presents, demands a renewal of proof of his integrity and manliness. Thus, Romero emerges as a young bullfighter whose principles and experiences have compounded themselves to form a steel-hard inner core of manhood.

The superiority of Romero's manhood proves itself not only in bullfighting but in sparring as well. In his encounter with Robert Cohn, he was physically mangled, but his spirit remained whole; his inner core of manhood remained untouched, unbroken, despite physical ruin. Hence, there was moral victory behind his physical defeat.

> "It seems the bullfighter fellow was sitting on the bed. He's been knocked down about fifteen times, and he wanted to fight some more. Brett held him and wouldn't let him get up. He was weak, but Brett couldn't hold him, and he got up. Then Cohn said he wouldn't hit him again. Said he couldn't do it. Said it would be wicked. So the bullfighter chap sort of rather staggered over to him. Cohn went back against the wall."
>
> "So you won't hit me?"
>
> "No," said Cohn. "I'd be ashamed to."
>
> "So the bullfighter fellow hit him just as hard as he could in the face, and then sat down on the floor. He couldn't get up, Brett said. Cohn wanted to pick up and carry him up and carry him to the bed. He said if Cohn helped him, he'd kill him, and he'd kill him anyway this morning if Cohn wasn't out of town. Cohn was crying, and Brett had told him off, and he wanted to shake hands. I've told you that before." (Mike related)
>
> "Tell the rest," Bill said.

> "It seems the bullfighter chap was sitting on the floor. He was waiting to get strength enough to get up and hit Cohn again. Brett wasn't having any shaking hands, and Cohn was crying and telling her, and she was telling him not to be a ruddy ass. Then Cohn leaned down to shake hands with the bullfighter fellow. No hard feelings, you know. All for forgiveness. And the bullfighter chap hit him in the face again." (Mike continued to relate)
>
> "That's quite a kid," Bill said.[1]

In the above passages, therefore, it is clearly shown that Cohn, despite the physical triumph he achieves, has been morally smashed to pieces and reduced to a "whimpering child"[2] by the integrity and unbroken manhood of Romero. In the face of physical defeat, Romero has remained well-composed and morally undefeated through the juxtaposition of these two strengths – physical and moral – it is tacitly expressed that moral strength is given higher valuation as it asserts its superiority over that which is physical. There is, therefore, a margin of triumph in Romero's defeat and, indeed, a triumph which is of a higher rank and category, for it is essentially a moral one.

In almost every milieu of living, therefore, Romero is able to prove his integrity, discipline and independent manhood, for his knowledge of the truths of life has armed him with a capacity to comprehend that life constantly holds at stake man's dignity and

---

[1] Ernest Hemingway, The Sun Also Rises (New York: Charles Scribner's Sons, 1926), p. 202.
[2] Melvin Backman, "Hemingway: The Matador and the Crucified," Modern American Fiction, A. Walton Litz, Ed. (New York: Oxford University Press, 1963), p. 204.

manhood. However, on the surface of his overall moral invulnerability, there lay a point of weakness through which Brett has injected her warmly absorbing but poisonously destructive influence. When Brett invades his world and he favorably and emotionally responds to her call, he places on an insecure state everything that he represents. This constitutes Romero's emotional crisis. Fortunately, however, with a very sudden outgrowth of some positive morality on Brett's part, she sets Romero free, out of an impulse of not wanting to be "one of those bitches that ruin children."[1]

Because of this emotional involvement, Romero becomes submerged in the world of Brett. And it is during this very momentary stay of Romero in this disorderly world that he undergoes physical ruin. In this encounter with Cohn, he suffers injury, but one which is physical; however, the steel-hard core of his manhood shielded him and seized the progress of the injury which could have shifted from a physical to a moral course. When he finally becomes disentangled from Brett, he endeavors to bring about a self-purification in the bullring. To Romero, the bullfighting arena is a pure, clean, and orderly world. Bullfighting itself is a sacred ritual in which an honest, disciplined ordering of the details of life is accomplished. In it, therefore, he endeavors to accomplish a sacred self-purification which cleanses away the dirty damages he had incurred in the disorderly world of Brett. Thus –

> The fight with Cohn had not touched his (Romero's) spirit but his face had been smashed

---

[1] Ernest Hemingway, The Sun Also Rises (New York: Charles Scribner's Sons, 1954), p. 243.

> and his body hurt. He was wiping all that out now.
> Each thing he did with his bull wiped that out a
> little cleaner.[1]

Hence, although his spirit remained unbroken, Romero still endeavors to wipe away any physical stain which might mean an offense to his manliness and integrity. This he achieves by every honest, disciplined, graceful move he makes in the bullring that gives him the moral assurance of his unconquerable manhood. Hence, this allows him to walk proudly about the arena of life with integrity, manliness, and greatness!

Reaching now the highest order of values, Count Mippipopolous catches the highlights of character delineation. Count Mippipopolous is a personification of the last stage of the learning process. He appears as the image of a perfected "Jake," who has passed through all the stages of life. His statement – "I have been around very much. I have been around a very great deal"[2] – delicately implies that he had lived much. This becomes further accentuated when he says "I have been in seven wars and four revolutions."[3] This implication takes on a genuinely outspoken form when, later, in a conversation with Jake, the count says, "You see, Mr. Barnes, it is because I have lived very much that now I can enjoy everything so well."[4] From the Count's experiences in life, therefore, he has learned the way to sip utmost enjoyment from everything. He, therefore, always looks forward to

---

[1] Ernest Hemingway, <u>The Sun Also Rises</u> (New York: Charles Scribner's Sons, 1954), p. 219.
[2] Ibid, p. 60.
[3] Ibid.
[4] Ibid.

getting his money's worth for anything he pays for. His exchange of value principle, however, is positioned on a higher level of gradation than Bill Gorton's. For, unlike Bill who is willing to buy stuffed animals to sip some momentary joy from the illusion of paying for life, Count Mippipopolous would be willing to pay if, in exchange, he gets "live" not "stuffed" animals; for only through this can he get his money's worth. Stuffed animals are false illusions of life, and since his values demand an honest, unillusioned approach to all things, he denies acceptance of "stuffed animals" as a fair exchange for his money. His experiences, therefore, have trained his mind to distinguish between real life and its imitations.

Furthermore, out of his experiences, he was able to create his own values. Thus, he developed a keen taste for wine, women, and food, so much so that he could derive maximal enjoyment from them. Hence, he says –

> "You see, Mr. Barnes, it is because I have lived very much that now I can enjoy everything so well. Don't you find it like that?"
>
> "Yes, absolutely."
>
> "I know," said the Count. "That is the secret. You must get to know the values."
>
> "Doesn't anything ever happen to your values?" Brett asked.
>
> "No, not anymore."
>
> "Never fall in love?"
>
> "Always," said the Count.

"I'm always in love…"

"What does that do to your values?"

"That, too, has yet a place in my values."

"You haven't any values. You're dead. That's all."

"No, my dear. You're not right. I'm not dead at all."

We drank three bottles of champagne, and the Count left the basket in my kitchen. We dined at a restaurant in the Bois. It was a good dinner. Food had an excellent place in the Count's values. So did wine…[1]

Count Mippipopolous' arrow wounds are a token that he had been "there" in the arena of life's struggles, and his experiences, therefore, have patterned out his outlook in life and have enabled him to create his own values against which to gauge his way of life. As he trotted along from stage to stage, life must have asserted before him its conditions of pain, and with every assertion came his realization of what it really is. Hence, with every pain he must have received, there must have been a corresponding build-up in his morale, giving a strengthening nourishment to his manhood, until he has emerged to his present state of perfection in the formation of the Hemingway figure. Therefore, for his painstaking efforts to assert his superiority over life's odds, he has worthily paid for what he enjoys now. He has deservedly earned his way to his present state for which reason, he proves himself

---

[1] Ernest Hemingway, <u>The Sun Also Rises</u> (New York: Charles Scribner's Sons, 1954), pp. 60-61.

superior to Romero. Pedro Romero, in his assertion of his superiority over Nature in the bullring, already has a foreknowledge of the conditions of life and the stakes of the game. Hence, his attitudes somehow follow a definite pattern of discipline. He knows the consequences of every move he makes, thus, freeing him from an unreasonable anxiety. Count Mippipopolous, on the other hand, as has been presented as a perfected "Jake", must have stepped in this game of life with the virgin innocence of a catechumen, with no foreknowledge of life's conditions. His was still to discover what they are and what life is all about. He did not know what life has in store for him. He was completely ignorant of the outcome of every move he makes. For this reason, he is filled with a deep, unreasonable anxiety. For him, therefore, to have reached this perfected state is a meritorious accomplishment which transcends the moral status of Romero.

As an overall synthesis of the above discussions, therefore, we may link together the three characters discussed, and view them against the background of Hemingway's *Meaningful Existence* to determine the extent of their approximation to the philosophy. Jake Barnes becomes involved in the process of learning truths about life and ultimately, after several falls, arrives at a discovery and realization that, to be able to live life meaningfully, one must confine and content himself with the illusions which his capabilities can satisfy. His principles of stoicism, discipline and integrity have paved the way to this goal of self-realization and self-abnegation, though he achieves this only after a series of trials and pains. The story leaves him at a point when he is just about to start living in accordance with what this self-realization and self-abnegation demands. The novel, thus, closes with an implication that Jake has successfully graduated from his lessons in life and, hence, is now prepared to live life meaningfully. His life continues in the person of Romero. Being an "aficionado" who recognizes and shares the principles of Romero, Jake, now in the person of Romero, realizes the pointlessness of life and the disorderliness of the world. So, in his desire to deduce some meaning in life and impose some order in this world of chaos and great disorder, he resorts to bullfighting. For, in the bullfighting arena, with all the medium of orderliness, grace and discipline on which bullfighting is conducted, bullfighting offers him a promise of redemption of the world for it appeals to him as a pictorial representation of an orderly world. Through Romero's resources and craftsmanship, therefore, he can impose order upon this world so that it undergoes an evolution from a world of disorderliness to a world of beauty, grace and order! However, though Romero stands as a paragon of integrity, discipline, courage, intelligence, and craft, Jake cannot live forever in the person of Romero, for he cannot live forever in a world-of-make-believe. He wants to be realistic. He wants to face life with all its painful realities. He wants to go through his days morally unaffected by such pains. So, his life shifts to continue its existence in the person of Count Mippipopolous. And in the Count's existential nature, he reaches and achieves the perfected state of the Hemingway figure. For Count Mippipopolous had learned to face life's painful realities morally unmolested. Nothing ever happens to his values anymore. He had found "things which he cannot lose." He has lived much on account of which he could enjoy everything so well. Hence, this way he lives life fully and meaningfully. The novel leaves him not in an unfinished state but in a perfected one. Though his life be ended, he suffers no loss, for he has reached the goal of his existence. Self-realization and self-abnegation have been achieved, and he has discovered the meaning of life with maximum enjoyment!

CHAPTER VI

HEMINGWAY'S PHILOSOPHY OF MEANINGFUL EXISTENCE IN <u>A FAREWELL TO ARMS</u>

The world portrayed in <u>A Farewell to Arms</u> is an indifferent world, capable of bestowing to all its creatures nothing but a life of continuous strife. As in <u>The Sun Also Rises,</u> therefore, the odds of life are set at a constant. It is a world into which the lovers, Frederick Henry and Catherine Barkley, are thrown. It is a game where "they throw you in and told you the rules and the first time they caught you off-base they killed you."[1] It is, in fact, a world which is more harsh and more cruel to the very good and the very brave. "If people bring so much courage to this world, the world must kill them to break them, so of course it kills them. The world breaks everyone and afterward many are strong at the broken places. But those that will not break, it kills. It kills the very good and the very gentle, and the very brave impartially. If you are none of these you can be sure it will kill you too but there will be no special hurry."[2] The world, thus, has brutality and pain as its natural components. For this reason, it stirs in Frederick Henry an intense cynicism which draws him to a position of emotional detachment—an indifference towards anything associated with it, a non-caring attitude.

---

[1] Ernest Hemingway, <u>A Farewell to Arms</u> (New York: Bantam Books), p.245.
[2] Ibid., p.186.

This non-caring attitude or emotional detachment is implicitly revealed by the fact that Henry almost cut the last strips of thread that bind him to his family. He does not write his family and has reduced his association with them to the bare minimum of a sight draft. Even in his participation in the war, there is a margin of detachment, and it is an emotional one. The carnage in it does not upset him at all; he views it at an emotional distance. He acts as an indifferent narrator. Thus, he narrates with complete emotional un-involvement –

> At the start of the winter came the permanent rain and with the rain came the cholera. But it was checked, and in the end only seven thousand died of it in the army.[1]

He volunteered to serve in the war without any war ideals to support it, nor any personal motives that may have contributed to such action.

The clue to his non-caring attitude is given in the early part of the novel when he narrates thus –

> ...and the world all unreal in the dark and so exciting that you must resume again unknowing and not caring in the night, sure that this was all and all and all and not caring. Suddenly to care very much and to sleep to wake up with it sometimes morning and all that had been there gone and everything sharp and hard and clear.[2]

---

[1] Ernest Hemingway, A Farewell to Arms (New York: Bantam Books), p.2.
[2] Ibid. p. 9.

The last line, however, shows that he has somewhat a very "strong potential for caring."[1] This potentiality becomes nursed later by Catherine with whom Henry falls so deeply involved in caring through love.

In the early part of the novel, Henry's non-caring attitude confines him in a state of self-detachment. He plays the game of life without any feeling of involvement. He even feels that the war will not kill him for it has nothing to do with him. He, thus, feels completely apart from it. However, this outlook on things of the world, which are synthesized into the incidents of the war, does not stay permanently with him. This outlook changes when he gets blown up at the Isonzo, north of Piave during an Austrian trench-mortar explosion. As he recounts –

> I tried to breathe but my breath would not come and I felt myself rush bodily out of myself and out and out and out and all the time bodily in the wind. I went out swiftly, all of myself, and I know I was dead and that it had all been a mistake to think you just died. Then I floated, and instead of going on, I felt myself slide back. I breathed and I was back.[2]

The passage "…. I knew I was dead and that it had been a mistake to think you just died," gives a very subtle revelation of Henry's discovery of a death-in-life, essentially, a moral death, in which he had remained submerged until this incident. He realizes he

---

[1] Earl Rovit, "The Structure of the Fiction," Ernest Hemingway (New Haven, Connecticut: Twayne Publishers, Inc., 1963), p. 100.
[2] Ernest Hemingway, A Farewell to Arms (New York: Bantam Books), p. 41.

has a self with which the war has something to do,[1] that he is a part of the war specifically, and of the world, in general. He discovers, moreover, that in this game which he plays, he has a self and a life at stake. This self-discovery and realization of life's value come to him during this shuddering experience at the Isonzo and after the incident, as he feels the drip of warm blood from a wounded hemorrhaging soldier lying on a canvas above him in the ambulance.

Henry's self-realization could be taken also as being dramatically represented when his soul gets out of his body, and takes an objective look of its dead body, which may be a concrete representation of the moral death he had had prior to this incident. Realizing the state of death in which his body lies, it slides back into its physical nature and accordingly, Henry is brought to a state of self-realization or self-discovery.

The soul becomes incorporated with caringness. Before the shocking Isonzo incident, the soul, the anima which imparts life, resides in Henry's body. Henry, however, suppresses and chokes it; thus, it could not manifest its existence fully. In view of this, Henry, accordingly, does not live life fully. During the Isonzo incident, Henry's soul gets out of his body, takes an objective look of its bare physical nature, devoid of its "self" and eventually realizes its body's complete death. As it slides back into its physical substance, the latter resumes its existence. Henry, therefore, is made to realize that it is the soul that imparts life to the body making it feel and realize its existence. Since it has been divulged in the quoted passages that Henry suffers

---

[1] Earl Rovit, "The Structure of the Fiction," Ernest Hemingway (New Haven, Connecticut: Twayne Publishers, Inc., 1963), p. 101.

from moral death through living in non-caringness or absence of caring, Henry, therefore, realizes that "caring" plays a potent role in the full existence of the soul – and thus, to the full realization of life and of meaningful existence.

Catherine Barkley is the emblem of caring, of love, of life. Before Frederick Henry achieves his self-realization at Isonzo, he takes his affair with Catherine as likened to a game of bridge. He feels emotionally uninvolved as could be perceived in his objective and detached manner of narration, thus –

> I turned her so I could see her face when I kissed her and I saw that her eyes were shut. I kissed both her shut eyes. I thought she was probably a little crazy. It was alright if she was. I did not care what I was getting into. This was better than going every evening to the house for officers where the girls climbed all over you and put your cap on backward as a sign of affection between their trips upstairs with brother officers. I knew I did not love Catherine Barkley nor had any idea of loving her. This was a game, like bridge, in which you said things instead of playing cards. Like bridge you had to pretend you were playing for some stakes. Nobody had mentioned, what the stakes were. It was alright with me.[1]

During the incident at Isonzo, however, he gets a very sharp idea of the stakes in the game of life he is playing. As has been mentioned, he realizes he has a self which the world and the war have something to do with, and a life which death can destroy. With this self-discovery comes, therefore, the realization that he should care for the

---

[1] Ernest Hemingway, A Farewell to Arms (New York: Bantam Books), p. 22.

world as he is a part of it.

His acquaintance with Catherine becomes warmer and more tender as his confinement in the hospital becomes prolonged. This acquaintance ripens into a tenderly blissful love which penetrates deeply into Henry's dormant and suppressed emotional being. The prolonged acquaintance, thus, opens the gateway to Henry's caringness. He becomes more and more involved in it and feels that a new world has been opened to him. Yes, a new world has been opened to him because amid the chaotic world in which he is, Catherine patterns out for him an idyllic world of self-fulfillment, mutual love, and happiness. This created world, they share together. Henry's past life of individualism, therefore, undergoes a process of evolution. He advances a step towards socialism; for instead of living a life of loneness and non-caring, he opens his life for another individual to share. Hence, Henry ceases to live alone in the vast world of the "rest," for a world for two is fashioned by Catherine for both of them. Consequently, he lives and struggles no longer alone, for there is Catherine to share his life and to take part in his struggles. Thus, Catherine says, "… because there's only us two and in the world there's all the rest of them. If anything comes between us, we're gone and then they have us."[1] They, therefore, confine themselves within this idyllic created world of theirs, struggling to preserve themselves from the world of others which they envision as full of pain, treachery, and gloom. Since their life, their love and their world are wholly set amid the vast world atmosphere of gloom, they could be likened to a

---

[1] Ernest Hemingway, <u>A Farewell to Arms</u> (New York: Bantam Books), p. 104.

flickering candlelight amid the cold mist of a threatening stormy night. As the flame struggles to keep itself alive, so these two lovers struggle to breathe, in union, the breath of life, the breath of love and self-fulfillment which make them realize the real meaning of life and the true feel of meaningful existence. Thus, Catherine says to Henry "Why, darling, I don't live at all when I'm not with you," and Frederick Henry replies, "I'm no good when you're not there. I haven't any life at all anymore."[1]

It is evident, therefore, that, though Frederick Henry's caringness is carried over only to one object of love, through it, he realizes his being and can sip some meaning from his existence.

Frederick Henry's individualistic tendencies reach their peak of manifestation as he abandons his army during the Caporetto retreat. He works out a "separate peace" in his "baptismal plunge" into the Tagliamento where he strips away all the symbols that show his attachment with the army, and emerges as a new man afterwards, as he roams the streets in civilian clothes. He goes to Stresa and resumes a life of bliss with Catherine in their own fashioned world.

Henry's act of removing all the stars of his uniform and, afterwards, going in civilian clothes, is a concrete representation of his separation from the army and all its ideals. His "baptismal plunge" into the Tagliamento ritualizes his severance from all his duties and obligations to organized society which is represented by the army. And as he emerges in civilian clothes and paves his way to Stresa to look for Catherine, he walks on bare of everything that represents the army

---

[1] Ernest Hemingway, <u>A Farewell to Arms</u> (New York: Bantam Books), p. 224.

and, thus, he has stripped off his old "self" and arises as a new person. From this point on, he follows the path of complete individualism, with Catherine as an extension of himself.

Henry's escape from organized society reiterates itself once more in his escape to Switzerland with Catherine. From then on, he and Catherine live together in their own world, uninvolved with the rest of the world.

Catherine Barkley, as has been mentioned, is the symbol of life. It is so because she portrays the series of pains which life presents. She is the dramatic representation of the continuous struggle in life. She suffers the pain of separation when she lost her first lover in the war; she takes upon herself all the sacrifices associated with her affair with Frederick Henry; she suffers the pain at childbirth; and finally, she suffers the pain of death. Moreover, she is life as life is incorporated with her being and with the breathing child she carries in her womb. Eventually, she is life, as is subtly implied in her great antagonism and struggle against death. Since life is antagonistic toward death, hence, Catherine, the symbol of life shows a great hatred and antagonism toward death.

Catherine finally becomes the soul of Frederick Henry, for it is through her, in "caringness" that Henry feels the true essence of life. She fashions a world of self-fulfillment, love, and happiness for Frederick Henry amid the world of disorder in which Henry lives. This is concretely represented by Catherine's act of building a clean, orderly and delightful home atmosphere for Frederick Henry.

Catherine is the dove of caringness because its true essence is found in her. The priest characterizes love – the truest form of caringness – in the following manner: "When you love you wish to do things for, you wish to sacrifice for, you wish to serve."[1] Following the priest's line of thought, it is doubtless that Catherine complies with these requisites of love. She wishes to make Frederick Henry happy at all costs. Even at childbirth, amid her painful labor, she still wants to prove to Henry that she is a good wife, endeavoring to give him no trouble at all. She wants to sacrifice alone, not even wanting to give Henry a piece of worry or mental torture. She remains lovingly sweet to show she is alright, and she often urges Henry to go out and eat, when behind her sweet smiles runs the bitterness of pain. She, therefore, stamps every pain with the seal of love, making her bolder as every pain comes along. As she becomes weaker, however, she feels disappointed and ashamed of herself, feeling she is giving Henry too much trouble. Thus –

> "I'm just a fool, darling," Catherine said. "But it doesn't work anymore." She began to cry. "Oh, I wanted so to have this baby and not make trouble, and now I'm all done and all gone to pieces and it doesn't work. Oh, darling, it doesn't work at all ...."[2]

Even as Catherine approaches the close of her life, therefore, her words and ways suggest that she is filled with the essence of love, sacrifice and service for the object of her love. This essence of caringness, defined by the priest and embodied by Catherine becomes infused to a certain degree into Henry's mind. During Catherine's

---

[1] Ernest Hemingway, A Farewell to Arms (New York: Bantam Books), p. 55.
[2] Ibid, p. 240.

delivery, Henry wishes to serve her or to do anything for her. Thus, Henry anxiously asks her "Do you want me to get a priest or anyone to come and see you?" and later, "Do you want me to do anything, Cat? Can I get you anything?"[1] And somehow, he feels happy to be allowed to do something for Catherine. Hence, when the doctor tells him to manipulate the gas apparatus for Catherine, he says to himself "It was so good of the doctor to let me do something."[2]

Since Catherine Barkley is the symbol of life, Henry's association with her establishes for Henry an association with life. And, as she later becomes Henry's very soul that imparts meaning to Henry's existence, her death has deprived the man of all meaning in life. Consequently, as Henry leaves the hospital, he walks in the rain to face a world of non-meaning. It is a world of non-meaning because the object of his love, the embodiment of caringness that makes his existence meaningful has left him. However, Catherine's death enables Henry to recognize the stakes in the game of life which he plays, for it has left him a "self" rendered vulnerable to the pains of life. He is led to a realization that he is part of the world, and that the world has something to do with him. And as he feels lost and robbed of all meaning in his existence upon the death of his object of caringness, he is made to realize, moreover, that it is in caringness that one achieves a meaningful existence.

When Frederick Henry was working on his "separate peace," he was running away from his responsibilities and was working on an uninvolvement in all of life's pains. His blissful life with Catherine

---

[1] Ernest Hemingway, A Farewell to Arms (New York: Bantam Books), p. 248.
[2] Ibid, p. 236.

serves only as a momentary interlude in the continuous struggles and pains which life presents. When Catherine dies, Henry realizes that he cannot escape the ills of life for they are part of the world to which he is attached. He is, thus, left to understand that he should not lead a life of uninvolvement or non-caringness for he has a self which the world can injure. The torture he suffers from Catherine's death is an adequate comment on the silliness of his attempt to escape life's pains through "separate peace". Moreover, such torture enables him to atone for his mistakes. That he is able to accept life's odds calmly and boldly is implied by the fact that it is he, not another, that realizes the story of his own life. This calm and bold acceptance of the series of pains that life presents gives him that sense of dignity, for he is somehow able to hold on and carry himself well despite life's odds.

The death of Catherine does not nullify the lesson gained by Henry. It has, in fact, moved him from the position of half-man—wherein his non-caringness has freed him from the anxiety of losing, but has disabled him to have a true feel for life. He realizes that it is through being maximally exposed and vulnerable to life's pains that he is able to live a fully human life.

CHAPTER VII

HEMINGWAY'S PHILOSOPHY OF MEANINGFUL EXISTENCE IN <u>FOR WHOM THE BELL TOLLS</u>

In <u>A Farewell to Arms</u>, the painful consequences of Frederick Henry's "separate peace" forecast the message conveyed in the dying words of Henry Morgan in <u>To Have and Have Not</u> which runs as follows – "No matter how a man alone ain't got no bloody… chance."[1] These words betray the Hemingway hero's realization of the absurdity of individualistic struggle. The message conveyed serves as a prelude and anticipation of the path of life which the forthcoming Hemingway heroes would take.

Hence, the next novel, <u>For Whom the Bell Tolls</u>, marks the advent of a new Hemingway hero, whose mature view of life governs his actions. His life is propelled by certain ideals which divulge a growing social concern. The point of greater concern, therefore, shifts from the "self" of the earlier heroes to the world outside of the "self" which this new hero purposes to achieve. Thus, there is a widening up of his visual field of concern, with his greater interest focused more on the common good than on his personal welfare. This attitude imparts nobility in his character and draws from him a certain degree of sacrifice.

Robert Jordan, the protagonist of the novel, moves forward to

---

[1] Ernest Hemingway, <u>To Have and Have Not</u> (New York: Charles Scribner's Sons, Inc. 1937), p. 248.

take this noble path of life. He voluntarily enlists in the Loyalist campaign for the cause of human liberation. Such voluntary gesture to become part of an organized society to fight for a noble cause offers a striking contrast and an act of atonement for the earlier Hemingway figure's (Frederick Henry's) act of disentanglement from the army, an organized society.

What propels Robert Jordan to an active participation in the war is his belief in the ideals it embodies. He takes the whole enterprise as the cause of human liberation, the success of which would mean man's freedom from oppression. Because he believes that the common good occupies a foremost position in man's concern, he gives away his life in defense of the noble cause. Thus, for the first time, the Hemingway hero emerges to inflate his heart with a genuine desire to sacrifice for mankind! Hence, Robert Jordan contemplates –

> It was a feeling of consecration to a duty toward all of the oppressed of the world which would be as difficult and embarrassing to speak about as religious experience and yet it was authentic…"[1]

And later, he adds –

> It was something that you had never known before but that you had experienced now, and you gave such importance to it and the reasons for it that your own death seemed of complete unimportance; only a thing to be avoided because it would interfere with the performance of your duty. But the best thing was that there was something you could do about this feeling and

---

[1] Ernest Hemingway, <u>For Whom the Bell Tolls</u> (Australia: Penguin Books Pty. Ltd., 1941), p. 225.

this necessity, too, you could fight.¹

And still much later he says as he recounts his past experiences –

"You learned the dry-mouthed, fear-purged, purging ecstasy of battle and you fought that summer and that autumn for all the poor in the world, against all tyranny, for all the things that you believed in and for the new world you had been educated into. You learned that autumn, he fought how to endure and how to ignore suffering in the long time of cold and wetness, of mud and of digging and fortifying. And the feeling of the summer and the autumn was buried deep under tiredness, sleepiness and nervousness and discomfort. But it was still there and all that you went through only served to validate it. It was in those days, he thought, that you had a deep and sound and selfless pride…"²

Jordan's participation, therefore, in the war demands a genuine sacrifice on his part. However, it is a sacrifice which Jordan willfully takes upon his shoulders for his "self" is pushed to the rear of importance by the nobility and value of its cause. He feels that it is this for which he is born. He, therefore, has a purpose for existence, a reason for living since he lives to accomplish this mission. He knows that meaningful existence could only be achieved by fulfilling his reason for living. When he is, thus, given the mission to blow up the bridge, he sets all his devotion, dedication, and efforts to the performance of this duty. Hence, the performance of this duty through

---

[1] Ernest Hemingway, For Whom the Bell Tolls (Australia: Penquin Books Pty. Ltd., 1941). p. 226.
[2] Ibid, p. 227.

which he could achieve his mission becomes his primal concern, bringing down in subordination any other activity that comes to his attention. This, he conveys in one of his conversations with Pilar, thus—

> "It is that I am very preoccupied with my work." (Jordan says)
>
> "But you do not like the things of life?" (Pilar asks)
>
> "Yes, very much. But not to interfere with my work."
>
> "You like to drink, I know. I have seen."
>
> "Yes, very much. But not to interfere with my work."
>
> "And women?"
>
> "I like them very much, but I have not given them much importance."[1]

Robert Jordan's devotion to duty, remains firm and unwavering despite his foreboding that his task to blow up the bridge would be futile. Prior to the scheduled day for the bridge, his observations point out to the futility of his mission. Despite the knowledge that his immediacy with the vital details of the situation supplies him with a better opportunity to have a keener and better study of the real situation, he works in accordance with the orders of his

---

[1] Ernest Hemingway, <u>For Whom the Bell Tolls</u> (Australia: Penguin Books Pty. Ltd., 1941), p. 89.

superiors despite his presentiment of doom, instead of working independently, basing his steps and strategic judgment on his individualistic study of events. This act of Jordan reveals a renunciation of individualistic struggle. He is conscious he is working with a team so he should learn to back his play in accordance with its rules and the agreement of its members. Thus, Jordan carries on his duty with the mystical faith that any "sacrifice of life that at all hinders the enemy, however, ineffectually, must promote the good cause merely because it has behind it his wholehearted enthusiasm as a subjective potential."[1]

Robert Jordan continues the life of caringness initiated by Frederick Henry in A Farewell to Arms. In fact, his caringness broadens its scope. Not only does he focus on one object of caringness—Maria, as the object of his love—but to a wider scope that includes the whole of mankind. When Jordan gives away his life for Maria, he is giving his life away for mankind because Maria is the emblem of life and of regenerative Nature.[2] Because Maria is the innocent victim of cruel oppression, Jordan's kind tendance of her which brings her back to wholeness makes Jordan the symbol of justice. As the cause of human liberation, represented by Jordan, heals the wound of oppression, and sets the oppressed to a new beginning, so Jordan, through love, opens for Maria a new life of hope. Maria represents life and regenerative nature. This is conveyed by Jordan's

---

[1] Edwin Berry Burgum, "The Psychology of the Lost Generation," Ernest Hemingway: The Man and His Works, John K.M. McCaffrey, ed. (New York: The World Publishing Company, 1950) p. 343.
[2] Melvin Backman, "Hemingway: The Matador and the Crucified," Modern American Fiction, A. Walton Litz, ed. (New York: Oxford University Press, 1963), p. 206.

way of calling her "rabbit" and by her cropped head, being referred to as a "field of growing wheat."[1] Moreover, Jordan considers her as "all of life" to him: "But in the night he woke and held her tight as though she were all of life and it was being taken from him. He held her, feeling she was all of life there was, and it was true."[2]

Eventually, Maria becomes the soul of Robert Jordan. For, even after death, Jordan believes he continues his existence in the person of Maria. Hence, at death, Jordan persuades Maria to go and escape, thus –

> "No, guapa, don't," he said. "Listen. We will not go to Madrid now but I go always with thee wherever thou goest. Understand?"
>
> She said nothing and pushed her head against his cheek with her arms around him.
>
> "Listen to this well, rabbit," he said. He knows there was a great hurry, and he was sweating very much, but this had to be said and understood. "Thou wilt go now, rabbit but I go with thee. As long as there is one of us there is both of us. Do you understand?"
>
> "Nay, I stay with thee."
>
> "Nay, rabbit. What I do now I do alone. I could not do it well with thee. If thou goest then I go too. Do you not see how it is? Whichever one there is, is both."

---

[1] Ernest Hemingway, <u>For Whom the Bell Tolls</u> (Australia: Penguin Books Pty. Ltd., 1941), p. 264.
[2] Ibid.

"I will stay with thee."

"Nay, rabbit. Listen. That people cannot do together." Each one must do it alone. But if thou goest then I go with thee. It is in that way that I go too. Thou wilt go now, I knew for thou art good and kind. Thou wilt go now for us both."

"But it is easier if I stay with thee," she said, "It is better for me."

"Yes, therefore, go for a favor. Do it for me since it is what thou canst do."

"But you don't understand, Roberto. What about me? It is worse for me to go."

"Surely," he said. "It is harder for thee. But I am thee also now."

She said nothing.

She looked at him and he was sweating heavily and spoke now, trying harder to do something that he had never tried in all his life.

"Now you will go for us both," he said. "You must not be selfish, rabbit. You must do your duty now."

She shook her head.

"You are me now," he said.

"Surely thou must feel it, rabbit. Rabbit, listen," he said.

"Truly thus I go too. I swear it to thee."[1]

And later, he adds, "Now thou art obeying not me but us both. The me in thee. Now you go for us both. Truly. We both go in thee now. This I have promised thee."[2]

In the above passages therefore, it could be perceived that Jordan incorporates himself with Maria. He identifies himself with Maria, for which reason, as Maria is the emblem of "regenerative Nature" he and the code he represents achieve immortality.

Furthermore, Maria is also the symbol of youth, and is taken as the lost youth of Pilar. For this reason, Pilar feels a very strong affinity and sympathy for Maria.

For Whom the Bell Tolls marks the end of despair and futility which served as the dominant motif in Hemingway's earlier novels. It serves as the pivotal novel from negativism to positivism because of the affirmative values it embodies. Sacrifice, so it conveys, is not futile if it is incorporated with a noble significance or intention like those which tend to the social good or to the defense of political belief or convictions. Even in the death of Jordan, the brave protagonist approaches it with courage and meets it with an affirmative outlook. Thus, he says to Maria in his final words to her – "Thou wilt go now rabbit. But I go with thee. As long as there is one of us, there is both of us."[3] And, a little later, he says as he contemplates alone, "If this attack

---

[1] Ernest Hemingway, For Whom the Bell Tolls (Australia: Penguin Books Pty. Ltd., 1941), p. 436.
[2] Ibid., p. 437.
[3] Ibid, p. 436.

is no good another one will be."¹ Moreover, this affirmative outlook in life is shown in the way Jordan views the world. Thus –

> The world is a fine place and worth fighting for and I hate very much to leave it. And you had a lot of luck, he told himself, to have had such a good life. You've had just as good a life as grandfather's though not so long. You've had as good a life as anyone because of these days.²

The accomplishment of Jordan's mission to blow up the bridge on schedule ends up being robbed of all meaning for the military scheme of the Loyalist Campaign. The whole activity seems to have been turned to complete futility because the Fascists have already prepared themselves for the attack; hence, they have already brought their reinforcements up the road. This situation, therefore, removes the blowing up of the bridge from being the pivotal center from which the whole future of the war and of the "human race can turn." This point of seeming meaninglessness could have induced a reiteration of the motif of futility of man's efforts. However, because the activity to blow up the bridge on time has been pulled down to insignificance, the focal point of significance shifts to the confrontation of the mission. It is this confrontation, ennobled by the whole band's courage and unity in spirit and action that imparts meaning on the futility and meaninglessness of the whole activity. The explosion of the bridge is, thus, meaningless only insofar as it gives no military aid to the Loyalists; notwithstanding this, it becomes meaningful since the bravery and united action of the

---

¹ Ernest Hemingway, For Whom the Bell Tolls (Australia: Penguin Books Pty. Ltd., 1941), p. 442.
² Ibid, p 440.

guerilla band, including Jordan, spells out the determination of humanity to live life with courage, dignity and meaning. The members of the band, being representative of the ideals of the Cause, integrate themselves into the mystical body of "Robert Jordan," the emblem of the Cause, who will stand as the immortal figure like the "earth that abideth forever!"

The discipline, with which Jordan carries out his mission at the sacrifice of his life, reveals the presence of a strong political conviction— a belief, in certain ideals which are taken with greater regard and value than life itself. It discloses Jordan's true dedication to duty – a trait which is alien to the earlier Hemingway protagonists. The united effort of working for a noble Cause suggests the spirit of fraternity or brotherhood among men. This sacred human relation lurks in Robert Jordan, thus, putting him in a state of tension and anxiety whenever he takes the life of another man. Thus, when he aimed at the sentry at the foot of the bridge, he felt that "his fingers were heavy with reluctance."[1]

> Robert Jordan felt his own breath tight now as though a strand of wire bound his chest and, steadying his elbows, feeling the corrugations of the forward grip against his fingers, he put the oblong of the foresight, settled now in the notch of the rear, onto the center of the man's chest, and squeezed the trigger gently.[2]

The same feeling seizes Anselmo, such that when he killed one

---

[1] Ernest Hemingway, For Whom the Bell Tolls (Australia: Penguin Books Pty. Ltd., 1941), p. 408.
[2] Ibid.

guard, "tears were seen running down his cheeks through the grey beard stubble."[1]

Robert Jordan and Anselmo, therefore, feel an indignation for killing. They only kill due to the call of duty. Anselmo, being the embodiment of man's innate goodness, anxiously demands for an atonement or for some penance which would wash away the guilt of killing. He takes killing as a grievous "sin" which "we have no right to do even though it is necessary."[2] He thirsts for an opportunity to atone for that sin.

Robert Jordan, as well as Anselmo, feels an unbearable heaviness of heart to kill another because he feels one with John Donne that "no man is an Island, entire of itself; every man is a piece of the Continent, a part of the Maine.... any man's death diminishes me, because I am involved in Mankind; and therefore, never send to know for whom the bell tolls; it tolls for thee!"

Through John Donne's immortal lines, therefore, flows the message that the same great concern that one gives to himself should be given to others because for every loss in others, he suffers an equal loss. Robert Jordan's commitment to the war to liberate a great number of oppressed must have been motivated by this principle. Hence, even before death, Jordan suffers no regret for he realizes that "life is worth living and that there are causes worth dying for."[3]

---

[1] Ernest Hemingway, <u>For Whom the Bell Tolls</u> (Australia: Penguin Books Pty. Ltd., 1941), p. 409.
[2] Ibid., p. 192.
[3] Philip Young, <u>Ernest Hemingway</u> (Minneapolis: University of Minnesota Press, 1959), p. 17.

CHAPTER VIII
HEMINGWAY'S PHILOSOPHY OF MEANINGFUL EXISTENCE IN
THE OLD MAN AND THE SEA

<u>The Old Man and the Sea</u> marks the culmination of the development of Hemingway's philosophy of Meaningful Existence. Frederick Henry's life of individualism in <u>A Farewell to Arms</u> had met its end upon Harry Morgan's realization of the futility of individual efforts in <u>To Have and Have Not</u>. This realization led to the complete occlusion of the individual efforts in <u>For Whom the Bell Tolls</u>, and the futility of individual struggle is once more reaffirmed, with a greater feeling of conviction in <u>The Old Man and the Sea</u>.

The nature of Frederick Henry's individualism is one of his own choice and decision; whereas, in <u>The Old Man and the Sea</u>, the individualistic struggle of Santiago is not out of his own accord, but one brought about by necessity. In fact, when Santiago fights the fish alone, he feels much the absence of the boy, Manolin, and he longs for the boy's presence. In his lone and hard struggle against the sharks, he feels the importance of human companionship and realizes that it is not really fishing that keeps him alive, though it supplies him his biological needs, but the love and care of another – the kind tendance of a companion who can keep his spirit up and his heart consoled in moments of pain and distress. Thus, he says, "Fishing kills me exactly as it keeps me alive. The boy keeps me alive, he thought. I must not deceive myself too much."¹

Santiago's individualism, therefore, simply rests on a very superficial plane. He is only individualistic as he struggles to kill and conquer the giant marlin alone. But his mental set-up does not concur with the individualistic struggle which he undertakes since he yearns for the presence of the boy, Manolin. His thoughts, therefore, essentially tends toward interdependence and solidarity.

The horizon of Santiago's spirit of solidarity widens up to include not only man but the whole of created life. He undoubtedly feels love for his fellowmen and respect for human struggle. However, this admirable quality does not limit itself to humanity. For, Santiago feels conscious of the existence of all creatures around him. He feels them part of his existence for they are united to him in sharing the pains of life. They share a common world together and each, therefore, contributes to the wholeness of the universe in which they all live. For this reason, Santiago has compassion for even little creatures like the birds.

Thus, with a feeling of kindness and intimacy, he speaks to a bird which perches on his fishing line, "Take a good rest, small bird. Then go in and take your chance like any man or bird or fish."² Man, bird, and fish may stand as the terrestrial, aerial, and aquatic representations of all creatures in the universe; and Santiago's statements, therefore, express the common ground on which all creatures stand. The same feeling of intimacy imbued with a warm

---

[1] Ernest Hemingway, The Old Man and the Sea (New York: Charles Scribner's Sons., 1952), p. 117.
[2] Ibid, p. 61.

sense of brotherhood bind Santiago with the rest of the created world. Thus, he says of two porpoises that come near his boat, "They are good. They play and make jokes and love one another. They are our brothers, like the flying fish."[1] Moreover, of the great marlin that he caught, he says, "I wish I could feel the fish. He is my brother."[2]

It could be noted, however, that Santiago's sense of brotherhood is extended only to those creatures that show some simplicity or nobility. This fraternity is blunted and turned to antagonism when he faces the scavenger sharks. The reason for this will be given a little later.

Santiago stands as a figure of the "Matador and the Crucified." He is the matador as he poses himself to kill the giant marlin. Yet, he is also the Crucified for all the sufferings he has patiently borne during the series of encounters he has undergone. As the bullfighter, therefore, fights with courage and dignity in the bullring, Santiago also fights with courage and dignity in the arena of life, the naturalistic world. Were the fight of the bullfighter in the bullring to be compared with Santiago's fight in the middle of the sea, it would be just to say that of Santiago deserves greater admiration. In the bullring, the theatrical atmosphere lends artificiality to the whole enterprise. One may even suspect that the bullfighter might already be undergoing a process of moral breakdown but that he only refuses to show its symptoms to the public for fear of dishonor. So, chances are that he performs with an outward look of firmness of spirit, courage, and dignity while beneath such

---

[1] Ernest Hemingway, <u>The Old Man and the Sea</u> (New York: Charlles Scribner's Sons., 1952), p. 61.
[2] Ibid, p. 67.

appearance lies a crushed moral spirit. With Santiago's lone struggle, this suspicion shall never confront anyone's mind. For, having no rational spectator to comment on every move he makes, any admirable act he executes all by himself, and any nobility of character he elicits, could not be mistaken for an artificial, theatrical display! Hence, there is a more reliable assurance of sincerity in all his actions.

As the bull in the bullring is an embodiment of Nature, presenting before the bullfighter the brutalities of Nature, likewise, the marlin in the sea takes upon itself the same role, thus, posing before Santiago the challenging power of the brute animal that represents nature. In both animals, Nature's strength is embodied; therefore, they both offer a challenge for man's endurance, seeming to explore man's craft and capacities of strength and forbearance. The physical strength, the challenging courage, and the unwillingness to accept defeat which impels both animals to fight to the last, impart a sense of nobility in them, thereby inciting in both bullfighter and Santiago the feelings of reverence and love for their opponents. Despite those feelings, both men are compelled to kill their respective opponents. For it is through this way that they prove triumphant over nature; it is through this way that they prove the superiority of man over the forces of Nature. This is what they are born for. This is the purpose of their existence. This is the motivation that drives them to face even the risk of death; the desire to prove man's superiority over Nature, such that even in the face of physical ruin, man's unwillingness to accept defeat drives him to achieve moral triumph which gives dignity and integrity to his manhood and imparts meaning to his existence.

In both bullfighting and fishing, death preys upon both man and animal. With a single carelessness or lack of skill on the part of the bullfighter or fisherman, death may capture him. However, if he works with full precision, skill, courage, craftsmanship, and intelligence, he dominates death itself, placing it under his control, making him the administrator of death himself. Death becomes under his command and when to administer it depends on his decision. When the bullfighter puts death into the bull, the enterprise ends there, for his triumph is achieved. In Santiago's fight with the fish, however, death occurs in two forms – in abstract form and in physical form. The death described above exists in its abstract form. In the bullfight arena, it is only this abstract form of death that exists. In Santiago's fight in the sea, however, the two forms of death occur. The abstract form has been explained in the preceding lines. The physical form, on the other hand, appears in the embodiment of the scavenger sharks. Hence, in Santiago's struggle, the fight moves one step farther than that of the bullfighter's. For, while in bullfighting the enterprise ends with the successful administration of death into the animal, in Santiago's fight with the fish, the enterprise does not end up with the killing of his fish. He encounters two forms of death and with the killing of the fish, he conquers the abstract form of death. However, the appearance of the scavenger sharks places him on another encounter with death – now in its physical form. The scavenger sharks are symbolic of death because of the violence and destruction which they bring on him and on the marlin. Also, his abhorrence for and his antagonistic attitude towards them show the same abhorrence and antagonism with which he faces death. When Santiago conquers the sharks, once again, he can assert his superiority over death. In view of this and of the greater struggle which Santiago faces, and of the consequent successes he earns, along with other reasons, he occupies a nobler and higher position than that of the bullfighter and deserves greater compassion and admiration.

The Old Man and the Sea shows the culmination of the evolution of Hemingway's moral views. It opens the alleys to greater hope in and reverence for man's struggle. In contrast to Hemingway's earlier novels, which depict a universe without a Creator, this book presents a universe with a Creator, who is neither hostile nor beneficent, but mysteriously just." Thus, the coming of the sharks is an adequate expression of the punishment he deserves for having gone too far, beyond man's true place in life. Hence, he feels that "the shark was not an accident."[1] "Yes, it was not an accident for it was a consequence of his killing the fish. The thrust of the harpoon into the marlin's heart caused the issuance of blood which left a track for the sharks."[2]

At the beginning of Santiago's struggle with the fish, he feels guilty, since he believes he used trickery to capture the fish. Hence, he enjoys no feeling of achievement or pride. Thus, he says, "I am only better than him through trickery and he meant me no harm."[3] He feels this way because he believes that "his (the marlin's) choice had been to stay in the deep dark water far out beyond all snares and traps and treacheries. My (Santiago's) choice was to go there to find him beyond

---

[1] Ernest Hemingway, The Old Man and the Sea (New York: Charles Scribner's Sons, 1952), p. 110.
[2] Clinton S. Burnhans, Jr., "The Old Man and the Sea: Hemingway's Tragic Vision of Man," Hemingway and His Critics, Carlos Baker, ed. (New York: Hill and Wang, Inc., 1961), p. 262.
[3] Ernest Hemingway, The Old Man and the Sea (New York: Charles Scribner's Sons, 1952), p. 110.

all people. Beyond all people in the world."[1] He becomes aware, therefore, of the sinfulness of his act, infusing into him a growing feeling of remorse when he killed the fish. Thus, he says, "I am sorry that I killed the fish."[2] However, he rationalizes in order to defend himself, thus, "you did not kill the fish to keep alive and sell for food – you killed him for pride and because you are a fisherman."[3] Notwithstanding this, the sinfulness of his act keeps confronting him until, eventually, he acknowledges it, and in a fit of remorse, speaks out a warm apology to his noble catch, half of which this time has already been devoured by the hungry sharks, thus–

> "Half fish," he said. "Fish that you were. I am sorry that I went too far out. I ruined Us both..."[4]

Beyond his triumph in his individualistic struggle with the fish, therefore, awaits his destruction for such triumph would only leave him nothing but the pain of losing the noble fish which he has learned to love and respect, and whom he has begun to identify with himself. This suffering, however, which is the measure of the punishment given him, widens up his moral vision that in man's individualism, in his pride, and in his need, he inevitably goes far out beyond the place where he should live, not knowing that in such venture, he will meet the pain and agony of failure bringing destruction and violence not only on himself but also on others. However, such venture is indispensable, for it is only

---

[1] Ernest Hemingway, The Old Man and the Sea (New York: Charles Scribner's Sons, 1952), p. 55.
[2] Ibid., p. 114.
[3] Ibid., p. 116.
[4] Ibid., p. 110.

"through the isolated individualism and the pride which drive him beyond his place in life does man develop the qualities and the wisdom which teach him the sin of such individualism and pride and which bring him the deepest understanding of himself and of his place in the world."[1] This constitutes the tragic irony of man's fate for man needs to undergo a state of sinfulness and receive an adequate punishment before he learns to understand himself and his place in the scheme of human existence. Therefore, man's voyage to that region where he is to receive the wisdom necessary to have a profound understanding of human existence, though bound up with sinfulness and agony, is morally enriching for it brings about an ennobling vision of man!

The campaign against individualism portrayed in The Old Man and the Sea is symbolized in various forms. In the earlier works of Hemingway, the sports that engage important characters are bullfighting and hunting – sports which demand individualistic struggle and yield individualistic success. Whereas, in The Old Man and the Sea, baseball which demands the united efforts of a team, is what catches the attention and interest of Santiago. A baseball team is composed of several members, each of whom shares a common interest and purpose with the rest, and works for the success, not of himself alone, but of the whole team. In this game, the failure of a member affects the whole and the success of one is the success of all! The united efforts, therefore, of the members of the team to work and struggle together to earn for the entire team the trophy of success, is an active,

---

[1] Clinton S. Burnhans, Jr., "The Old Man and the Sea: Hemingway's Tragic Vision of Man," Hemingway and His Critics, Carlos Baker, ed. (New York: Hill and Wang, Inc., 1961), p. 266.

pictorial metaphor of human solidarity and interdependence. And since this is the specific sport that preoccupies the mind of Santiago, it may be taken as expressive of the spirit of solidarity and interdependence which the novel indoctrinates. Unlike the earlier novel, <u>The Sun Also Rises</u>, in which the protagonist adores the bullfighter, Santiago in <u>The Old Man and the Sea</u> idolizes DiMaggio, the great baseball player who wishes not to stand out alone to make himself conspicuous within the group, but who works not for his personal interest and success but for those of the group to which he belongs. DiMaggio attracts Santiago in a very special way because, despite the bone spur in his heel, he can endure his pain and still achieve greatness. Santiago's thought of DiMaggio's endurance and greatness sustains him during his trying, difficult struggle in the sea and gives him an added vigor and spirit to bear his pain. Hence, every time he encounters difficulty with the fish, his mind turns to the great DiMaggio and the thought of this noble baseball player consoles him and renews his strength. Santiago's long and painful struggle in the sea inclines him towards hopelessness and despair; however, his belief that "it is silly not to hope"[1] sustains him. As food for his moral spirit, therefore, he assures himself that were the great DiMaggio in the same situation as his, he would also "stay with a fish as long as I will stay with this one."[2]

    Solidarity and interdependence are also symbolized in Santiago's dream of the lions on the beach.

    He no longer dreamed of storms, nor of women, nor

---

[1] Ernest Hemingway, <u>The Old Man and the Sea</u> (New York: Charles Scribner's Sons, 1952), p. 115.
[2] Ibid, p. 75.

of great occurrences, nor of great fish, nor fights, nor
contests of strength, nor of his wife, ---

The only dream that remains with him now is that of the young lions playing on the yellow beach. The past dreams were symbolic of individual ventures, with the selfish motive of earning personal success. The only remaining dream now – the young, peaceful, happy lions on the yellow beach – gives a panoramic impression of solidarity and interdependence. It is a dream which gives impressions of tranquility, harmony, and brotherhood, a dream devoid of the violence, selfishness, and individualism of the past ones.

As Santiago stays far out in the sea, he languors for a companion. However, noticing the wild ducks flying overhead, he feels that "no man was ever alone on the sea."[1] In the absence of a man-companion, therefore, he feels some joy and consolation in having some other forms of created life around him. A sense of need for them is, thus, implied, feeling them part of his existence.

The old man himself, stands as a personification of the universe. His eyes are blue, like the sea and the sky; his hands are scarred like the eroded sterile desert; his skin has been browned by the sun – all the vital parts of Nature or of the universe namely the sky, the land, and the sea, have been carefully represented and unified in the person of Santiago. And since these body parts of Santiago are vital for his wholeness, for the completion of his physical being, and furthermore, since such body parts particularly his hand, unitedly work

---

[1] Ernest Hemingway, The Old Man and the Sea (New York: Charlles Scribner's Sons., 1952), p. 115.

together to enable Santiago to achieve and enjoy a meaningful existence, the shown interdependence of Santiago's body parts to complete his physical being and give meaning to his existence points out to the interdependence of the represented parts of the universe.

The world portrayed in The Old Man and the Sea is one which is kinder than that portrayed in the earlier works of Hemingway. Santiago describes his town as a "good town" where people show deep concern, interdependence, and brotherhood. Pedrico, the wine shop owner; Martin, the restaurant owner; and Manolin, the boy – supply the old man's biological needs. And when Santiago approaches the shore after having been away from home for long, he surmises that the boy and the rest of his townmates must have been worried – a surmise which shows some faith in the innate goodness and loving concern of the people in his own world. And, finally, reaching his shack, he enjoys the same warm and kind tendance from the same people. Manolin cries over his lacerated body and brings him some food and wine which Pedrico and Martin have kindly offered.

At the close of the novel, he notices "how pleasant it was to have someone to talk to instead of speaking only to himself and to the sea,"[1] and realizing this, he tells the boy "I missed you."[2] This touching utterance which comes from the old man's heart is an expression of the old man's regret for having "gone too far out, beyond all people," and is, therefore, a delicate comment on the emptiness of individual struggle.

---

1 Ernest Hemingway, The Old Man and the Sea (New York: Charles Scribner's Sons, 1952), p. 137.
2 Ibid.

The Old Man and the Sea circles around man's moral values. Courage, love, humility, solidarity, and interdependence are effectively interwoven within the Saga of Santiago, seasoned by the admirably delicate symbolisms in the novel. Only when man lives in accordance with these moral values can he achieve a Meaningful Existence.

CONCLUSION

It is indeed remarkable that behind the simplicity of Ernest Hemingway's language and characters lies the profundity of his philosophy. If a careful analysis of Hemingway's major novels from the first to the last be conducted, such technique would inevitably draw a distinct line of development in Hemingway's moral philosophy.

This <u>Conclusion</u> embodies a Christian evaluation of Hemingway's Philosophy of Meaningful Existence. Moreover, it endeavors to trace the phases of his philosophy from his first major novel to his last. In view of this, pertinent points found in every novel which may substantiate the achievement of this purpose will be carefully delineated.

To be able to trace the development of Hemingway's philosophy, therefore, let us first consider <u>The Sun Also Rises</u>.

In <u>The Sun Also Rises</u>, the milieu within which the characters move is a "moral wasteland". Love, the very root of Christian charity, is an impossibility. It lives in the heart of Jake Barnes, but his impotence kills it and drives him to complete individualism. It is a love which is rich but is bound to be isolated, for it resides within a man whose physical condition disables him to manifest it; moreover, it happens to have been directed to a woman whose nature cannot accept its limitations. Hence, it is a love so true and yet isolated in one; individualistic, for it cannot be shared by two. It is only possible for one who cannot act in accordance with its normal practices. The only love possible, therefore, is still driven to extinction for it is an illusion from which Jake, the lover, must detach himself. Jake is, thus, taught to live only by those things which his capabilities permit.

In The Sun Also Rises, love is thus doomed from the start and the hopeful efforts of the lovers for the realization of love is met with a degree of mockery because of a foreknowledge of its doom. In A Farewell to Arms, however, despite the tragic end of love, love's fate is not determined beforehand. The lovers managed to keep its flame burning despite the dampened atmosphere in which it flickers. They have unitedly, carefully, and tenderly kept it burning and they would have been successful in their attempt to keep it forever burning had not Catherine's death interfered and appeared onto the scene. Hence, while in The Sun Also Rises love is fatalistic, in A Farewell to Arms, love's tragic end is not anticipated. It is accidental. In The Sun Also Rises, there is no gleam of hope for love from the start; whereas, in A Farewell to Arms, there is an affirmation of hope in love, and as the novel progresses, love becomes more blissful and promising and would have continued its happy course had it not been for Catherine's death. But Catherine's death is still part of the whole scheme of love; it is part of the game of life and of love that the lovers are playing. Love in A Farewell to Arms is, therefore, still cruel for it takes the form of a biological trap that lures the lovers by its bliss and destroys them once they are in. However, despite its tragic implications, A Farewell to Arms is still emotionally and morally richer than The Sun Also Rises for it leaves a margin of enjoyment to the bitter suffering borne in love. For, in The Sun Also Rises, there is suffering in love all throughout the novel; whereas in A Farewell to Arms, enjoyment and bliss in love seem to reign throughout the novel except in the end where love makes its tragic pose! The tragedy of love, though felt but once in <u>A Farewell to Arms</u>, is felt more severely than it is felt in <u>The Sun Also Rises</u>; however, the way the lover, Henry, is made to experience love is more morally wholesome, thereby integrating the moral being of Frederick Henry. For, while in <u>The Sun Also Rises</u> Jake is saved by his physical incapacity from the more painful experiences in love, Henry, through living a love-life, experiences its greater pains, thus, becoming morally stronger. Through living life, he discovers its truths, experiencing its pains and pleasures— such that he eventually emerges as a complete person with a deeper understanding of what life is and how he can adapt to it.

Moreover, love progresses from its individualism in <u>The Sun Also Rises</u> to its mutuality in <u>A Farewell to Arms</u>. The lovers Frederick Henry and Catherine Barkley in <u>A Farewell to Arms</u> can share the bliss of love together. Each can reciprocate every gesture of affection which the other offers; hence, there is a mutual sharing of affection.

<u>The Sun Also Rises</u> depicts the harshness of life with resignation and stoicism. The attitudes of the characters take the course of escape. They run away from the cruel truths of life by forgetting about them. They avoid the problem. In <u>A Farewell to Arms</u>, the lovers meet the problem; they face and try to solve it unitedly; they do not run away from it, but instead, confront it with unbroken courage and determination; and though they escaped to Switzerland, it was not a "running away from the problem" but a means that they have thought to be able to preserve themselves and to realize their dreams, thereby enjoy a meaningful life. Their struggles, thus, involve an active participation in life. Contrasted with <u>The Sun Also Rises</u>' passive,

individualistic way of living, united effort seals the lovers' way of life.

The pervasive spirit of demoralization in The Sun Also Rises is adequately expressed in the general attitude of stoic acceptance of and resignation to all pains. This mood is delicately embedded in the settings which are generally dry. In all, except the bullfight and the sparring scenes, there is neither bloodshed nor violence. Occasionally, however, violence slips through the scenes and when it does, it reveals itself in a highly charged but disciplined and controlled fashion. Such is the nature of violence portrayed particularly in the bullfighting scenes; and the passion of Jake Barnes and the other members of the clique to witness such orderly violence is expressive of these peoples' desires to bring order and harmony to their unorganized lives. Their indifference to the scenes of bloodshed and death reflects their callousness to violence from which spring their attitudes of stoic acceptance and resignation to all pains in life.

Whenever the bullfighter successfully maneuvers and controls every thrust of violence offered by the bull, the aficionado, Jake Barnes, experiences a thrill. This is because the bullfighter's power to take rein of such violent charges quenches Jake's thirst for man to put violence under his control. The feeling of elation after witnessing a clean bullfight result because of witnessing a dramatic counterpart of life in the bullfight arena, with the dream of life completed and fulfilled and its elements successfully and adequately met. In Jake's true life, the elements of life are present but are not met properly and successfully; hence, from life, he can sip no enjoyment. In the dramatic presentation of life in the arena, life's elements are not only present but are properly and successfully handled; thus, a realization of some effects in the proper handling of these elements is fulfilled, thereby completing the process of stimulus — response — effect. Since the stimulus is present (life elements) man (bullfighter) responds; and since the response is proper and adequate, the effect is favorable, thus, enjoyment is achieved. In the drama of life in the arena, therefore, there is the achievement of enjoyment; eventually, there is fulfillment of a goal in life. In Jake's actual life, there is no such fulfillment, and, in the arena, he achieves this completion which in his own true life remains wanting. This is the root of his experience of elation; for even just by witnessing the drama of life in the arena, he somehow feels a completion of life.

The Sun Also Rises, therefore, pivots around the delicate sensing of the emotional turmoil of man in a state of complete disillusionment. Thus, in keeping with the demands of the novel's mood, a dry atmosphere is usually made to predominate. Bloodshed and violence are set to the minimum; chaos and destruction are of an emotional nature. There is external peace but within the emotional being of every individual, there is internal turmoil. It is this internal turmoil that keeps the characters of the novel, except Romero and Count Mippipopolous, restless. Cast against this atmosphere, A Farewell to Arms outlines its sharp contrast. For as The Sun Also Rises puts its emphasis on moral destruction, A Farewell to Arms stresses on physical destruction. The second novel is placed within the milieu of war, of bloodshed. Nevertheless, despite this predominant physical destruction, there is moral victory; for beyond physical defeat lies the lovers' unbroken spirit. There is, therefore, a morally progressive shift from The Sun Also Rises' complete moral sterility to A Farewell to

Arms' richer moral content. This moral content, however, is not sufficient to wash out the mud of demoralization that fills the scenes of A Farewell to Arms. For though love and mutual efforts are brought to a certain degree of affirmation, the other elements of life are treated with ironic sarcasm. Thus, Frederick Henry, losing faith in political ideals, says –

> I was always embarrassed by the word sacred, glorious, and sacrifice and by the expression in vain. We heard them... and had read them in proclamations, now for a long time, and I had seen nothing sacred, and the things that were glorious had no glory and sacrifices were like the stockyards in Chicago if nothing was done with the meat except to bury it.[1]

Moreover, the positive leanings of love are given an ironic twist at the end of the novel with Catherine's death. Thus, since the cruel conception of life in The Sun Also Rises is still carried over to A Farewell to Arms. The second novel, however, is morally richer since it casts out the attitudes of stoic acceptance and indifferent resignation to life's pains, which are very much present in The Sun Also Rises. It brings forth and stresses the elements of struggle and mutual effort, though such are eventually doomed. The mutual struggle is metaphorically represented by the flame of the lovers' love amid the threatening violence of a stormy night. Though the flame struggles to keep itself forever burning, the violent rain eventually extinguishes it. No wonder Catherine envisions herself as "dead in the rain."[2]

---

[1] Ernest Hemingway, A Farewell to Arms (New York: Charles Scribner's Sons, 1929), p. 137.
[2] Ibid, p.94.

In *A Farewell to Arms*, thus, as in *The Sun Also Rises*, Hemingway maintains a cruel perspective of life. As to the lovers, Jake and Brett, life is a chain of pains; to Henry and Catherine, it is a series of pitfalls which proves crueler and harder to "the good, the gentle, and the brave,"[1] for "The better you are, the harder it dealt with you."[2]

Thus far, the moral progress from the first novel to the second is barely felt; for the only visible progress is the evolution of love from promiscuity to a deeper emotion. This nature of love, which is placed mainly on the level of enjoyment, is not specifically a Christian love. However, its moral value lies in its capacity to incite mutual relationship and united effort and struggle.

The protagonist's isolated love in *The Sun Also Rises* is given freedom to express itself morally and be received and reciprocated favorably in *A Farewell to Arms* as love springs from the hearts of Henry and Catherine. Hence, in the second novel, love disentangles itself from isolation; it becomes reciprocal, inciting not an individualistic and egotistic effort but a mutual one for the happiness of both. This apparently shows a progressive step towards socialism. However, this would be a very weak point from which to conjecture a socialistic progress. For, both lovers struggle not for the good of society but for themselves. Frederick Henry struggles not for a particular concern for society (since he even abandoned the army for personal interests) but for the good of himself and of his own. Love has merged Catherine into his own being so that every struggle he makes has the sole goal of preserving the two of them, who exist as one, as Catherine

---

[1] Ernest Hemingway, *A Farewell to Arms* (New York: Bantam Books). p. 245.
[2] Ibid.

says, "I don't live at all when I'm not with you,"[1] and Henry confirms their united existence by saying "I'm no good when you're not there. I haven't any life at all anymore."[2]

In For Whom the Bell Tolls, individualism meets its end, for the tyro figure, Robert Jordan, shifts to solidarity and interdependence. This moral growth in the Hemingway tyro figure has been foreshadowed in the dying words of Harry Morgan in To Have and Have Not— "no man alone now… no matter how a man alone ain't got no bloody… chance,"[3] – words that express the futility of individual efforts. This realization, which is reached at the end of the novel, To Have and Have Not, is activated in For Whom the Bell Tolls. For, the tyro figure discards his individualistic "self" and enlists himself in the Loyalist Campaign in defense of the Cause of human liberation. The words that meant nothing to Frederick Henry in A Farewell to Arms are now the very words which impel Robert Jordan to action and sustain him in suffering. Jordan joins the war for political convictions which are alien to Frederick Henry. Henry joins the war for no reason at all, not even for any political cause; though physically involved in war, he feels personally uninvolved. Whereas Robert Jordan "fought now in the war because it has started in a country that he loved and he believed in the Republic and that if it were destroyed, life would be unbearable for all those people who believe in it."[4] Apparently, he joins

---

[1] Ernest Hemingway, A Farewell to Arms (New York: Charles Scribner's Sons, 1929), p. 224.
[2] Ibid.
[3] Ernest Hemingway, To Have and Have Not (New York: Charles Scribner's Sons, Inc., 1937), p. 130.
[4] Ernest Hemingway, For Whom the Bell Tolls (New York: Charles Scribner's Sons, Inc., 1940), p. 226.

the war not for any egotistic interest, but for the common good — a sudden offshoot of social concern in the Hemingway tyro figure.

The situations that led Frederick Henry to his desertion from the Italian army were not sufficient to drive Robert Jordan toward the same action. The confusion of the Loyalist forces approximates that of the Caporetto retreat, and the love affair that exists between Jordan and Maria is practically the same as that which exists between Henry and Catherine. Despite this, and despite the foreboding of death that comes to Jordan, he sticks with the army and accomplishes his mission. Impelled by political ideals, he offers his life as a sacrifice for the liberation of the oppressed and, at the hour of death, he suffers no regret because he believes that his sacrifice is not "in vain" since there are ideals which are worth sacrificing for. He suffers no regret for he feels he has accomplished his duty and has somehow defended the ideals of liberty and justice. And, lying on the cold ground, he awaits his death with a calm spirit and wholeheartedness for he believes that upon his death the values of liberty, justice, brotherhood, and interdependence shall reign and live an immortal life!

It would be noted that in contrast with The Sun Also Rises, love in A Farewell to Arms is fertile. Its fertility, however, is eventually ended by the element of accident in life. The cruel hand of life came as a pestilence that destroyed the mother-plant with her fruit when harvest time was on; Catherine died with her child during delivery. In For Whom the Bell Tolls, love is handled with affirmation. For, even as life closes to Robert Jordan, his image and code which he represents shall continue to live in the person of his child. This positive expectation of Jordan is delicately insinuated as he urges Maria to escape for he believes that wherever Maria is, there the two of them shall be; therefore, he hopes to continue his existence in Maria for Maria carries in her womb his flesh and blood and everything he represents.

In The Old Man and the Sea, Santiago is the Hemingway tyro, grown old. He is the perfected tyro because he is the product of the synthesis of all the earlier tyros together with their experiences. Hence, he is the wisest and the one who could endure most. He is the embodiment of the ideals of courage, patience, humility, integrity, solidarity, and interdependence.

In A Farewell to Arms, Hemingway asserts that defeat is inevitable. In To Have and Have Not, however, Harry Morgan realizes that the world is not to blame for his failure. He believes that he failed because he struggled alone. And in his dying words, he conveys the end of individualistic struggle, for he believes that "defeat is not inevitable" if man would work together in the struggle against the forces of Nature. The same belief is carried over to For Whom the Bell Tolls and is, in fact, the substantiating theme of the novel. With an enlivened hope, the Hemingway tyro, now in the person of Santiago, comes in The Old Man and the Sea to say that "man is not made for defeat. A man can be destroyed but not defeated."[1]

The Old Man and the Sea embraces a broader scope of interdependence. For, it does not only reveal human interdependence but interdependence among all created life.

The Old Man and the Sea, therefore, marks the pinnacle of Hemingway's moral development because, of all his literary works, it

---

[1] Ernest Hemingway, The Old Man and the Sea, (New York: Charles Scribner's Sons, Inc., 1937), p. 114.

is this novel which contains the most and the greatest of his moral values.

Inasmuch as this concluding chapter embraces a Christian evaluation of Hemingway's philosophy of Meaningful Existence, the focus will now be to pertinent points which show possibility of Christian evaluation.

The full essence of Hemingway's philosophy of Meaningful Existence demands that, for man to live life properly and meaningfully, he should live by the values of courage, endurance, dignity, humility, solidarity, and interdependence. The courage and endurance, however, which Hemingway requires his characters to have to be able to achieve meaningful existence, have lost the sense of moderation so that, instead of being virtuous, they become vicious. Christian fortitude demands a certain degree of moderation; that is, it must stand midway between the meek, soft, weak, and cowardly to preserve man from harm, and the necessary exposure to pain, if such is necessary for the attainment of a greater moral good, like the defense of one's rights. Hemingway's fortitude appears with an extreme exposure to pain and danger so that it approximates suicidal intentions.

Moreover, the Hemingway courage and endurance blend with pride and stoicism which are non-Christian elements; for while Christ pronounces the second Beatitude in the Sermon on the Mount "Blessed are the meek, for they shall possess the land," the Hemingway figure proudly fights and tries to conquer even nature itself. Even before death, their stoic attitude towards it springs from an innate pride. There is not even a trace of resignation to God's will in their behavior before death. And it is this kind of proud, unbroken spirit that Hemingway's people idolize. In Christianity, humility and awe fill the heart of the dying; there springs a certain fear for the coming Great Judgment. This fear is partly inspired by an inexplicable reverence for God, the Creator, but a feeling of trust in God's justice and love consoles the dying and fills him with great hope and faith in God's mercy. He thus submits himself completely to God's will since he acknowledges that God, being the giver of life, has the right to take it away. He experiences sorrow for all the sins he had committed against God; and finally, he willingly breathes forth his soul into the hands of his Creator. The true Christian, when in danger of death, contemplates on his appearance before God in the Divine Judgment. He conceives of a life hereafter and prays for eternal salvation. Hemingway's dying man does not have such thoughts. His concentration is laid on how to fight death or remain morally unbroken before it. He meets it with pride instead of humility and meekness. In none of Hemingway's novels is a next life ever conceived. There is no conception of a Final Judgment. Thus, since the Hemingway characters are only concerned with the "here and now;" they do not sacrifice a temporal good for their life is practically based on physical pleasure or, on temporal satisfaction.

In The Sun Also Rises, there is complete loss of ethical values. The characters do not look at things with divine interference. To them everything is the result of simple "exchange of values;" thus, Jake says – "No idea of retribution or punishment. Just exchange of values."[1]

In A Farewell to Arms, amid the moral and physical destruction, the characters still believe in the existence and interference

---

[1] Ernest Hemingway, The Sun Also Rises, (New York: Charles Scribner's Sons, Inc., 1926), p. 148.

of God. However, their relationship with God has rather waned to a low level, as though they considered God or the Blessed Virgin as mere comrades. Thus, a wounded Italian screams –

> "Dio te salve Maria, Oh Jesus shoot me. Christ, shoot me. Oh, purest lovely Mary, shoot me. Stop it. Stop it. Stop it. Oh, Jesus, lovely Mary, stop it. Oh, oh, oh!"[1]

Also, Frederick Henry prays to God for Catherine in the following manner:

> "Oh, God, please don't let her die. I'll do anything for you if you won't let her die. "Please, please, please, dear God, don't let her die. Dear God, don't let her die… God, please make her not die. I'll do anything you say if you don't let her die. You took the baby but don't let her die. That was alright but don't let her die. Please, please, dear God, don't let her die."[2]

In the above passages, it could be noted that the "exchange of value" metaphor of The Sun Also Rises is carried on to A Farewell to Arms. The way Henry pleads seems to give the impression that God is so business-like a Being at bestowing grace; that God demands that he should promise to do something in return or in exchange for his request, once granted.

Thus, though the Hemingway man acknowledges God's power to grant graces, his regard of Him is not akin to the way a true Christian reveres Him.

---

[1] Ernest Hemingway, A Farewell to Arms, (New York: Charles Scribner's Sons, Inc., 1929), p. 247.
[2] Ibid.

With regards to the attitude towards pain, the Hemingway man looks at the pains of life with indignation. And if he ever bears them, he does so stoically, feeling them inevitable, and at best, he bears them heroically with a tinge of sacrifice for a noble purpose. The sacrificial effort, therefore, in accepting the pains of life ends with the achievement of the noble purpose. The true Christian approaches every pain of life as a trial that tests his faith in God and the extent to which he can suffer for Him. He is not negativistic or indignant to pain because he looks at it from a religious angle. When misfortune crosses his life, he either looks at it as a trial about his religious faith, if his conscience is clear; or, as a punishment or a means of atonement for his sins, if he is guilty of any offense against God, which put his conscience in a state of remorse. He accepts the misfortune with a whole heart, taking it as a Cross which God wills him to bear. With this attitude, therefore, he feels some consolation in suffering because it gives him hope of reconciliation with God and of eternal salvation. In the presence of a clear conscience, suffering is still bound up with joy because, as it is taken in the name of the Lord, he feels happy to be in the service of God. This explains the essence of martyrdom. To the true Christian, this life is but a preparation for a next which is of greater importance. He, thus, aims toward the attainment of the perfect "good" that will unite him with God, and thereby, enjoy an immortal life of perfect happiness. This, as well as the essence of martyrdom, does not reside in the Hemingway character. All of Hemingway's characters are mundane. What they value is the "here and now." Hence, they live, as reflected especially in <u>A Farewell to Arms</u>, <u>The Sun Also Rises</u> and <u>To Have and Have Not</u>, for the gratification of the senses and the present exhilaration of joy. Unlike the Christian way of living, they have no vision of a next life; hence, their ways in this present life are not directed towards a life of spirituality. Consequently, their passions are not in any way subdued by virtues of chastity, temperance, and moderation. They do not exert effort at all to control their passions, but instead, they delight in the exploitation of them. This is because they live only for the present. In none of the earlier novels do the characters ever ponder on a life hereafter. Passions are hard to subdue and, unless an intention far nobler and significant, like the call of religious duty, be attached to the sacrifice of abstaining from them, it would be of no sense to get committed to the sacrifice. Since practically all of Hemingway's early novels have been presented in a state of religious and moral catastrophe, the characters bear the imprint of such condition. Thus, as the Hemingway hero tries to perfect himself through the series of experiences he undergoes, the true Christian tries to perfect himself by directing all his action and impulses toward the path of the good and the just.

Hemingway's principle of morality calls for an involvement in an experience before one realizes what it is. If it gives him pleasure, it is good; if not, it is bad. This principle is not in conformity with the Christian concept of morality. For, according to Hemingway "an action is good if it makes one feel good after, and an action is bad if it makes one feel bad after;" to the Christian, an action is good if it is in accordance with the "law of life."

The true Christian believes in the innate goodness of man because man is created after the image of God, the Greatest Good. As has been discussed in Chapter II, man elicits no tendency away from the good; he commits an evil act not for its own sake but for reasons which his perverted mind sees as right. God infused into man's nature the sense of the good which takes the form of the conscience. The conscience is the faculty or "internal recognition of right and wrong as regards one's actions and motives."[1] It, thus, guides man in his way of life and helps him to fight against evil and follow the good and the just path of life. Evidently, therefore, ethical morality has its germ infused into man's nature. It is not formed by experience as what Hemingway asserts, but on the contrary, it is that which guides man's actions. To the Christian, it is the "determinant" of experience, not the "consequence" of experience. Vincent Martin, O.P. says, "there are certain fundamental goods, certain basic values which man discovers rather than makes. According to St. Thomas, man sees and recognizes that it is morally good to protect his life, to have a family, to possess property, to love the truth or to practice the virtues; and man, also sees and recognizes that it is morally evil to wantonly destroy human life, to inflict undue injury on other human beings, to be cowardly, to become a slave to his passions. It is not man who makes life good or truth worthwhile. It is not man who makes murder an evil, or slander something foul, rather he recognizes that they are evil and foul."[2]

Hemingway's concept of morality is based on "pleasure;" the Christian concept is based on the norm of "the good and the just." It would place one on a weak stand should he take pleasure as the

---

[1] C.L Barthart, and others (eds.), The American College Dictionary (New York: Random House, Inc.), p. 257.
[2] Vincent Martin, O.P. Existentialism (Washington 17, D.C.: The Thomist Press, 1962), pp.24-25.

determinant of morality; for the narrowness and transience of pleasure make it an unsound basis for a far broader and more permanent concept like morality.

In For Whom the Bell Tolls, however, Hemingway's philosophy of Meaningful Existence becomes richer in Christian elements, thereby, making it closer to the Christian philosophy of Meaningful Existence. It shares the Christian principle that, to live properly and meaningfully, man should not only be concerned with his duties to himself, but also with his duties to others and to God. Robert Jordan makes a sacrifice for his fellowmen. Thus, he says "you (may) do nothing for yourself but perhaps you could do something for another."[1] And, "you have put many things in abeyance in order to win a war."[2]

Furthermore, his belief that "no man has a right to take another man's life unless it is to prevent something worse happening to other people,"[3] is in accordance with Christian teachings. This belief prevents him from assassinating Pablo and gives him a feeling of reluctance and sadness when he kills the cavalryman by force of duty. This act of killing drives him to a state of agitation and initiates a long examination of conscience about his right to kill. This nature of Jordan moves him closer to Anselmo; for Anselmo has the same attitude towards killing and is filled with the desire to be able to accomplish his duties without necessarily taking the life of another. Anselmo's innate goodness is

---

[1] Ernest Hemingway, For Whom the Bell Tolls, (New York: Charles Scribner's Sons, Inc., 1940), p. 439.
[2] Ibid., p. 289.
[3] Ernest Hemingway, For Whom the Bell Tolls (Australia: Penquin Books Pty. Ltd., 1941). p. 439.

revealed as he often ponders on atonement. Thus, he says–

> I wish there were a penance for it that one could commence now because it is the only thing that I have done in all my life that makes me feel badly when I am alone. All the other things are forgiven or one had a chance to atone for them by kindness or in some decent way. But I think this of the killing must be a very great sin I would like to fix it up.[1]

And earlier, he says –

> I think that after the war there will have to be some great penance done for the killing. If we no longer have religion after the war then, I think, there must be some form of civic penance organized that all may be cleansed from the killing or else we will never have true and human basis for living. The killing is necessary, I know, but still the doing of it is very bad for a man and, I think, after all this is over and we have won the war, there must be a penance of some kind for the cleansing of us all.[2]

One of the reasons that enable Jordan to accept his death courageously and with dignity is also the spirit of atonement. His father committed suicide, an act which is a grievous violation of the Hemingway Code. To make the code live, therefore, Jordan must wipe out the sin of his father, and in a spirit of atonement, he faces and accepts his death with courage and dignity. His death, therefore, is a sacrifice: firstly, for a noble cause; secondly, to wipe out the stain of

---

[1] Ernest Hemingway, <u>For Whom the Bell Tolls</u> (Australia: Penguin Books Pty. Ltd., 1941), p. 192.
[2] 2 Ibid, p. 288.

his father's cowardice; and, thirdly, to make the "Code" live. Henceforth, his sacrifice is not in vain, for with his death comes the reincarnation of the "code" by which he lived. However, the spirit of atonement that drives Jordan "to die fighting" is one which is accomplished to refute suicide inclinations and to wash away the sin committed by his father. Hemingway's approach in achieving the atonement varies with the Christian approach. Suicide is, for both the Hemingway and the Christian principles, a sin. Nevertheless, while the Hemingway hero washes it away by fighting, which is expressive of pride and strength, the true Christian atones for it by prayers and sacrifice offered for the love of God, a gesture expressive of humility and meekness.

Lastly, to compare Anselmo with Pablo, whose commitments to killing take the form of lust, these two people are antagonistic in various ways; for Anselmo and Pablo, respectively, represent "loyalty as against treachery, courage as against fear, gentleness as against cruelty."

The question of killing is carried over to <u>The Old Man and the Sea</u>. In this novel, killing also confronts the old man. Santiago ponders on whether killing is a sin. Thus, he says –

> Perhaps, it was a sin to kill the fish. I suppose it was even though I did it to keep me alive and feed many people.[1]

He kept on thinking about sin; and later, perhaps, to appease

---

[1] Ernest Hemingway, <u>The Old Man and the Sea</u> (New York: Charles Scribner's Sons, Inc., 1952), p. 116.

his troubled conscience, he says –

> You did not kill the fish only to keep alive and sell for food, he thought. You killed him for price and because you are a fisherman. You loved him when he was alive and you loved him after. If you love him, it is not a sin to kill him. Or is it more?[1]

Santiago's feeling of brotherhood not only for his fellowmen but for the rest of created life shows the very spirit of Christian love and charity. Moreover, his belief that the coming of the sharks is a just punishment for his sin of "having gone too far out beyond all people," and his acceptance of his loss of the great fish which he had sacrificed for and have learned to love, are reflective of the presence of Christian elements in the novel, such as punishment or retribution and atonement.

The <u>Saga</u> of Santiago or his voyage in the sea of life may be viewed from the standpoint of the Passion of Christ. As Santiago goes on his voyage of life, he encounters many sufferings along the way to reach the goal of his existence. Despite such sufferings, he goes on to achieve his mission in life, what he is born for, the reason for his existence, just as Christ takes the path of agony and suffering before He accomplishes His mission of redeeming mankind. Santiago follows Christ in the journey of life and, thus, like Christ, he journeys along with patience and endurance. Being a fisherman is what he is born for; and through the accomplishment of such a mission does he feed himself and the townspeople. Christ assumes the form of Man to redeem

---

[1] Ernest Hemingway, <u>The Old Man and the Sea</u> (New York: Charles Scribner's Sons, Inc., 1952), p. 116.

mankind and, like Santiago, through the accomplishment of His mission. He feeds Himself with happiness for reconciling mankind with God and, thereby, win back for man the kingdom of heaven; also, through the achievement of His mission, He feeds man with the knowledge of learning how to live a Christian life; and, essentially, He feeds their spirit with love, charity, and eternal happiness. In the footsteps of Christ, Santiago, worn out by much pain, falls, too, and the manner of his falling, with the fishing line over his shoulder producing several lacerations on his back and shoulders, show a very striking symbolical resemblance with Christ's fall under the heavy Cross. And, as Santiago walks to his shack with his mast on his shoulder, he falls again, and this picture gives a clearer and closer semblance with Christ's fall under the Cross. Reaching his shack, he lies face down with hands stretched out and his bloody palms up — a clear-cut replica of the Crucifixion.

Santiago embodies the virtues of humility, endurance, patience, love, and sacrifice — virtues which find their perfect expression in Jesus Christ, Himself. In view of this, Santiago widens the breadth of Hemingway's moral philosophy.

It is in <u>The Old Man and the Sea</u>, therefore, that Hemingway achieves a broadening of his moral horizons through the injection of Christian symbolisms into the novel.

In conclusion, the evolution of Hemingway's Philosophy of Meaningful Existence reached its culmination in <u>The Old Man and the Sea</u> where Hemingway shares a kinship with the Christian Philosophy of Meaningful Existence.

BIBLIOGRAPHY

Primary Sources:

A. BOOKS

Hemingway, Ernest. The Sun Also Rises. U.S.A. Scribner's Sons, Inc., 1926. 247 pp. _____. A Farewell to Arms. New York: Charles Scribner's Sons, Inc., 1947 363 pp. _____. For Whom the Bell Tolls. New York: Charles Scribner's Sons, Inc., 1940. 471 pp. _____. The Old Man and the Sea. New York: Charles Scribner's Sons, Inc., 1952. 140 pp.

Secondary Sources:

A. BOOKS

Baker, Carlos. The Mountain and the Plain: The Writer as Artist. Princeton, N.H.: Princeton University Press, 1956. Pp. 95-101;106-107_____. Hemingway and the Critics. New York: Hill and Wang, Inc., 1961. 276 pp.

Baugh, Albert Croll. Will David Howe and Arthur Hobson Quinn (eds.). The Literature of America. U.S.A. Charles Scribner's Sons, 1938. 1491 pp.

Benet, William Rose and Normal Holmer Pearson (eds.) The Oxford Anthology of American Literature, 2 vols.

Burgum, Edwin Berry. "Ernest Hemingway and the Psychology of the Lost Generation," Hemingway: The Man and His Works, ed. by John McCaffery. New York Publishing Company

Clark, Donal Lemen and Roger Sherman Leomis (eds.). Modern

English Readings. Fifth edition. New York: The Viking Press, 1947. 1043 pp.

Cowley, Malcolm (ed.). Hemingway. New York: Rinehard Company, Inc., 1944. 642 pp.

Dorey, J. Milnor. A Short History of the World. New York: Garden City Publishing Co., Inc., 1949. 240 pp.

Ellis, Milton and others (eds.). A College Book of American Literature. Second edition. U.S.A.: American Book Company, 1949. 1107 pp.

Fadiman, Clifton (ed.). The American Treasury. New York: Harper and Brothers, Publishers, 1955. 1108 pp.

Fenton, Charles A. (ed.). The Apprenticeship of Ernest Hemingway. New York: The Viking Press, 1954. 302 pp.

Fiedler, Leslie Q. Love and Death in the American Novel. New York: The World Publishing Company, 1964. Pp. XVIII, 125, 175, 186, 304-309, 321, 350-352.

Geismar, Maxwell. Writers in Crisis. Cambridge, Massachusetts, 1942.

Glenn, Paul J. Ethics. U.S.A.: B. Herder Book Company, 1952, Pp. 48-70

Heiney, Donald W. Essentials of Contemporary Literature. Barron's Educational Series, Inc., 1954. 503 pp.

Hoffman, Frederick J. "The American Novel Between Wars," The Modern Novel in America – 1900-1950. Chicago: Henry Regnery Company, 1951. Pp. 89-130

_____. The Twenties – American Writing in Post-War Decade. New York: The Viking Press, 1955. 466 pp.

Hull, Ernest R. Man's Great Concern: The Management of Life. New York: P.J. Kenedy and Sons, 1920. 176 pp.

Kazin, Alfred. "Hemingway: Synopsis of a Career," Hemingway: The

Man and His Works, ed. John McCaffery. New York: The World Publishing Company, 1950. P. 190

Litz, Walton (ed.). Modern American Fiction. New York: Oxford University Press, 1963, pp. 201-255

Martin, Vincent, O.P. Existentialism. Washington 17, D.C.: The Thomist Press, 1962. 48 pp.

Martindale, C.C.. Man and His Destiny. New York: The MacMillan Co., 1928. 85 pp.

McCaffery, John K.M. (ed.) Ernest Hemingway: The Man and His Works. Cleveland and New York: The World Publishing Company, 1950. 575 pp.

Millet, Fred B.. Contemporary American Authors. New York: Harcourt, Brace and Company, Inc., 1944. 716 pp.

Nyren, Dorothy (comp. and ed.). A Library of Literary Criticism. New York: Frederick Ungar Publishing Company, 1960. Pp. 227-231

Panizo, Alfredo. Ethics or Moral Philosophy. Manila: Novel Publishing Company, 1964. 347 pp.

Poore, Charles. The Hemingway Reader. New York: Charles Scribner's Sons, Inc., 1953. 651 pp.

Quinn, Arthur Hobson (ed.). Literature of America. New York: Appleton – Century – Crafts, Inc., 1951. 1172 pp.

Spiller, Robert, Ernest. The Cycle of American Literature. New York: The MacMillan Company, 1955. 318 pp.

_____. and others (eds.). Literary History of the United States. New York: The Macmillan Company, 1948. 816 pp.

Stallman, R.W., "The Sun Also Rises – But No Bells Ring" The Houses that James Built. U.S.A.: Michigan State University Press, 1961. Pp. 173-193

Throp, Willard. American Writing in the Twentieth Century. U.S.A.: Harvard University Press, 1960. 353 pp.

Trent, William Peterfield and others (ed.). The Cambridge History of American Literature. New York: The MacMillan Company, 1947. 676 pp.

Wagenknecht, Edward. Cavalcade of the American Novel. New York: Henry Holt and Company, 1952. 574 pp.

Warren, Robert Penn. "Hemingway," Literary Opinions in America, ed. Morton Dauwen Zobel. New York: Harper and Brothers, 1951. Pp. 444-463

West, Ray B.. The Art of Modern Fiction. New York: Rinehart Winston, Inc., 1949, pp. 622-633

Wilson, Edmund. The Wound and the Bow. New York: Oxford University Press, 1947. 295 pp.

PERIODICALS

Baker, Carlos. "Hemingway," Saturday Review, XLIV, No. 30 (July 29, 1961), pp. 11-13

_____. "A Man, A Writer, A Legend." Saturday Review, XLIV, No. 30. (July 29, 1961), Pp. 14-17

Bessie, Alvan C.. "Review of For Whom the Bell Tolls" New Masses, XXXV II, (November 5, 1940), Pp. 25-29; 135-136.

Betsky, Seymour, "A Lost Visit." Saturday Review, XLIV, No. 30 (July 29, 1961) Pp. 22-24

Colvert, James B. "Ernest Hemingway: Morality in Action." American Literature XXVIII, No. 3 (March 1956)

Ciardi, John. "Manner of Speaking." Saturday Review, XLIV, No. 30 (July 29, 1961), p.32

Halliday, E.M., "Hemingway's Ambiguity: Symbolism and Irony." American Literature, XXVIII, No. 3 (March 1956)

Hemingway, Mary. "Ernest Hemingway." Sunday Times Magazine, (October 22, 1961), Pp. 24-27

Patanne, E.P., (ed.). "Ernest Hemingway," Sunday Times Magazine, July 30, 1961, Pp. 13- 14

Cousin, Norman (ed.). "A Feeling About Life." Saturday Review, XLIV, No. 30 (July 29, 1961), Pp. 30-31

_____ "A Literary Sampler" Saturday Review, XLIV, No. 30 (July 29, 1961), Pp. 37-38

_____ "Milestones on Literary Journey." Saturday Review, XLIV, No. 30 (July 29, 1961), Pp. 27-29

_____ "The World Weighs A Writer's Influence." Saturday

Review, (July 29, 1961), Pp. 18-22

Hemingway, Mary. "Hemingway," Look Magazine, XXV, No. 19 (September 12, 1961) p. 22

Hicks, Granville. "Love and Death Hemingway," Saturday Review, (January 14, 1961), p. 15

Locsin, Teodoro M. "The Death and Art of a Twentieth Century Man," Philippine Free Press, (July 15, 1961), Pp. 2-3

Loeb, Harold. "The Young Writer in Paris and Pamplona." Saturday Review, XLIV, No. 30 (July 29, 1961), Pp. 25-26

Luce, Henry (ed.). "Brave Drama of Bullring Stirs Spain," Life Magazine, XXVIII No. 7 (September 28, 1959), Pp. 22-29

_____ "The Last Words Hemingway Wrote," Life Magazine, L1 (August 25, 1961) p. 7Manila, Quijano de. "Hemingway Was Here," Philippine Free Press

Moloney, Michael F.. "The American Novel Through Fifty Years: Ernest Hemingway." America. Pp. 1-4

Patanne, E.P. (ed.). "Ernest Hemingway," Sunday Times Magazine (July 30, 1961), Pp. 12-14

_____. "Spain No Like Papa Hemingway," Sunday Times Magazine, XVI, No. 33 (March 26, 1961), Pp. 20-21

Robin, A.. "Living Legends," Today's Health, XXXVIII (October 1960), p. 16

Roy, David (ed.). "A Talk on the Wild Side," The Reporter, XX, No. 12 (June 11, 1959) p. 31.

Sanford, Marcelline Hemingway. "At the Hemingways: Walloon Lake" The Atlantic (December, 1961) Pp. 31-39

Taylor, R.. "Fatalism," Philosophical Review, (January, 1962)

U.S.I.S.. "Kennedy, Literary Figures Pay Tribute to Hemingway" (July 5, 1961), Pp. 1-4

_____ "Death Comes to Ernest Hemingway." (July 3, 1961) Pp. 1-2

_____ "Death Comes to Hemingway." News Digest. (July 17, 1961) p.4 Young, Philip. Ernest Hemingway. No. 1 (1959), 43 pp.

www.ingramcontent.com/pod-product-compliance
Lightning Source LLC
LaVergne TN
LVHW051035070526
838201LV00009B/206